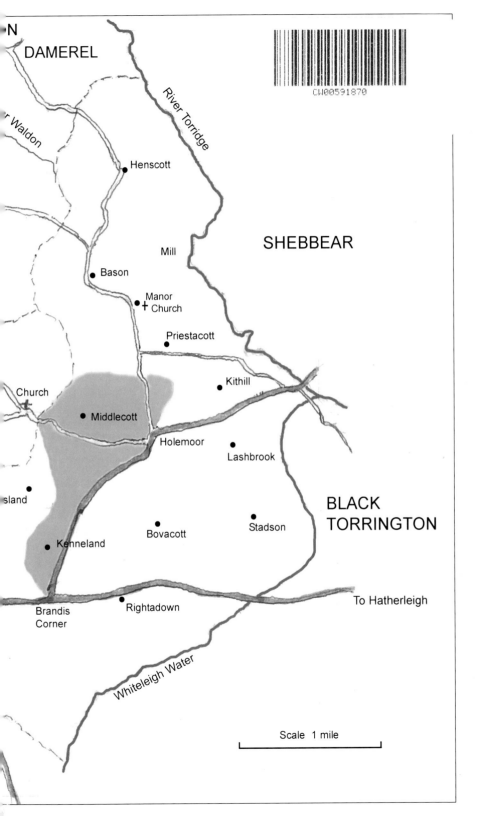

The Parishes
of

Bradford
and
Cookbury

A thousand years of history

Gerry Matthews
28 Nov. '12

Gerry Matthews

Edward Gaskell
DEVON

First published 2012
Edward Gaskell publishers
6 Grenville Street
Bideford
Devon
EX39 2EA

isbn 978-1-906769-01-7

© Gerry Matthews

The Parishes of
Bradford and Cookbury

Gerry Matthews

Typeset, printed and bound by
Lazarus Press
Unit 7 Caddsdown Business Park
Bideford
Devon
EX39 3DX
WWW.LAZARUSPRESS.COM

The Author

Gerald Matthews was born in Bridgwater, Somerset in 1931, and moved at an early age to Bridport in Dorset. He was educated at West Buckland School in North Devon, where he spent seven years, and Bristol University, where he read law and was a member of the Bristol University Dramatic Society. After two years' National Service with the Royal Signals Regiment he studied for ordination at Ripon Hall, Oxford and was made deacon by the Bishop of Birmingham in 1957.

He returned to the West Country as Vicar of Brent Tor in 1963 and in 1978 became Priest-in-Charge of Black Torrington, where he has remained, retiring from stipendiary ministry in 1990.

His interests include history, drama, collecting (and reading) books.

In 2003 he published Black Torrington The Second Millennium which was re-printed in 2011.

Lazarus Press
DEVON

CONTENTS

Above: Dunsland House circa 1950.

Below: Dunsland restored, circa 1960.

Bickford Arms, Brandis Corner, Bradford.
Before the age of the motor car.

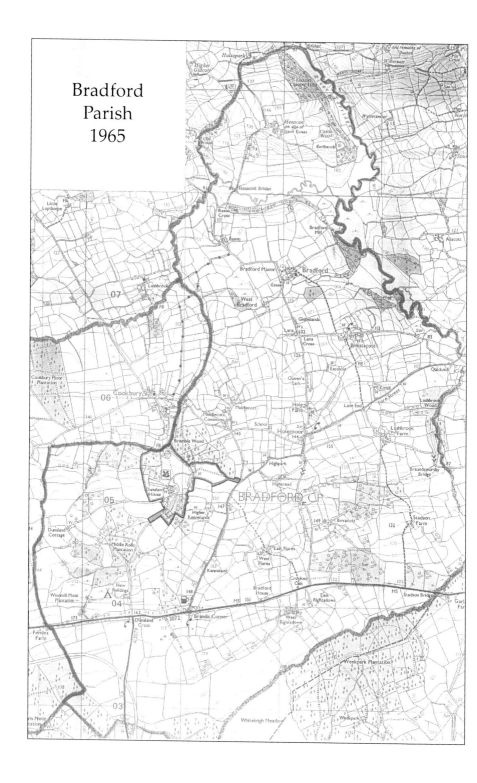

Bradford
Parish
1965

PREFACE

I could not have written this book as it is without the help of many others, especially those who supplied me with facts about the parish as they remembered it in their youth. In particular I would like to thank John Smale, Eileen Heard, Esther Griffiths, Marion Westaway, June Pennington and the late Bryan Reed for sharing with me their memories. I am also grateful to the late Grace Smyth for granting me access to some of the English family papers deposited at the Devon Record Office. I have taken many notes from "The Dunsland Saga" by the late Bickford Dickinson which was published posthumously in 1996 and is still available from the Churchwardens of Bradford.

I have been helped by the loan of many photographs: Nigel Manners for his copies from the English family albums, Sheila Granger, Alan Barnes, Maurice Thomas and Dennis Curno (not only for his own photographs but also for the loan from his collection of old postcards). I should also mention the late Brenda Tanswell whose Bradford W.I. calendar for 2000 revealed the existence of many of these photos.

Gerry Matthews.

August 2011.

INTRODUCTION

The guardians of the ancient parish churches of England are, or were, the custodians of a great many historical documents; not only the parish registers of baptism, marriage and burial, but also many other books. Some parishes have churchwardens' account books, occasionally going back to mediaeval times, but more often to the eighteenth century. They may also have had the account books of the Overseers for the Poor and, in the nineteenth century, the local rate books.

In the past clergy often used these as resource material when writing the history of their local church. Within a few years of my becoming Vicar of Brentor the guide book for St Michael's Church needed reprinting, so I began to review the contents, and to see where they could be improved or amplified; and I did this in every other parish of which I was incumbent.

I said at the beginning 'or were custodians'. This is because since the 1980s when County Record Offices began to get more organized, these Offices began to take custody of all the older registers – every book that was not still in use and was over 100 years old. The keeping of registers of baptism, marriage and burial in parishes was first ordered in 1538. Over eighty Devon parishes still have records going back to the 16th century, but only about fifteen which start in 1538. Those for Bradford are preserved from 1558. The Cookbury registers for Baptism and Burial were only preserved from 1746, and Marriage from 1813. All the registers for Bradford from 1558-1837 were transcribed in 1950 by Lt-Col. Ormiston of Exminster with an index, and deposited in the Exeter City Library, and a copy was given to the parish. He did this for a great many parishes throughout the County.

The earliest national record is the Domesday Book. This was compiled for William the Conqueror, listing every manor and its lord and tenant, so that the king could know what estates he owned and how much revenue was due to him. In 1841 a census of every person in the kingdom was compiled, giving their residence, age and occupation. In 1851 their place of birth was added, and a census has been made every ten years since then. The personal details are made public after 100 years. In 1839 the Tithe Redemption Act called for the mapping of every parish with the naming of the owners and occupiers of all the land and an assessment of the value. There were three copies of every map: one went to the Rector who was entitled to the tithe, one to the diocesan registry and one to the Tithe Commission (this one now being held by the National Archives at Kew). The parish copy for Bradford has not survived, but the diocesan copy is in the Devon Record Office.

Wills made by private persons down the centuries are also public documents once they have been granted probate. Before the 20th century only a minority of people left a will, and before 1858 these might be proved in a variety of courts, often in the ecclesiastical courts, and many have not survived. Many copies of wills which were stored in the Exeter City Library were lost in the blitz of Exeter in 1942; fortunately a number of them had been transcribed and these copies are still extant.

In the 18th century directories were published listing the names of the leading residents and commercial businesses in the greater cities. By the mid 19th century they began to be published taking in every town and village. William White published the first History, Gazetteer and Directory of Devonshire in 1850. This was followed by M. Billing's Directory in 1857. Kelly's County Directories were started in the 1850s and were reprinted every few years until 1939.

Court records, both civil and ecclesiastical, are another source of information, but are not indexed and therefore difficult to reference. The West Country Studies Library, in Exeter, has an excellent indexed file of early local newspapers, particularly useful is the *Exeter Flying Post* from 1763-1885.

This library also has an excellent collection of local manuscripts and all the census records for Devon.

Names and dates can cause some confusion. The Julian calendar which had been in use since the time of Julius Caesar was found to have serious faults and in the 16th century Pope Gregory XIII ordered a new calendar, known as the Gregorian, to be used throughout the Holy Roman empire from 1582. England was not going to be dictated to by a Pope and kept the old calendar until 1752. Hitherto the year was reckoned to begin on 25th March so that dates between 1st January and 24th March were part of what we would term the preceding year.

Because there was a discrepancy between the calendars of eleven days the day after September 2nd in 1752 was September 14th! This caused much worry, misapprehension and some riots as many people thought they were being cheated of eleven days of their lives!

Spelling was not very precise before the 18th century and people were not consistent even in the way they spelt their own names: Shakespeare is often given as an example of the various ways in which one could sign one's own name. Added to this is the fact that names in parish registers were written by the parish clerk who wrote as he heard and spelt according to his own fashion. Spelling of names in this book will also vary according to the documents from which they are copied.

I am aware that I have made references to the old style coinage (pre 1971) of pounds, shillings and pence, so perhaps I should remind the younger generation that one old shilling was equal to five new pence, and that there were twelve old pence to the shilling.

So we come in an untidy fashion to the long history of Bradford: an old place some four miles east of Holsworthy, straddling the Holsworthy – Hatherleigh road, with the parish church some two miles north of this road, standing 350 feet above sea level.

1

BRADFORD BEFORE THE CONQUEST

O nce upon a time there was a broad, or wide, ford across the river Torridge connecting the Saxon settlement of *Sceft Beara or Sepesberia* (Shebbear), with *Hengescote*, where the Saxon Hengist is reputed to have made a fortified settlement, overlooking the Torridge river east of Henscott. Whether Hengist, who was an Anglo-Saxon invader of Kent in the 5th century actually built here is a matter of conjecture for there is no evidence that he penetrated the Celtic kingdom of Dumnonia which comprised Cornwall, Devon and West Somerset. The battle of

The Torridge in Flood: View from Dipper Mill Bridge looking into Shebbear
(Photo: D. Curno)

Penselwood in 658 A.D. marked the beginning of the Saxon penetration into the West, which did not immediately get much beyond Exeter and took at least a century to cover most of Devon, or *Defena*, as it was called in 825 A.D.

Perhaps the ancient Bradford earthwork is contemporary with Durpley Castle near Ladford in the north of Shebbear, which is reputed to be originally a Danish fortification. The Danes captured Exeter in 876 A.D. and were in north Devon in 893. With much coming and going Wessex finally succumbed to Danish rule under Cnut in 1016. It did not last long, and fifty years later came the Norman invasion. The remains of the motte and bailey at Durpley are thought to be Norman work of the eleventh century. So the earthwork in the wood near Henscott may also be a Norman reworking of an earlier period.

All this is necessarily a matter of some conjecture, but the 'broad ford' gives a name to the ancient manor of **Bradefort**.

When William the Conqueror became king he wanted to know the extent of his wealth in the new kingdom, and who held lands and how much tax they were due to pay. This resulted in the publication in 1086 of a record of land holdings.

These facts were compared with the ownership and value at the time of the death of Edward the Confessor. This survey became known as the Domesday Book.

The Saxons had been good administrators and had formed the 'shires' over most of England by the 9th century. In turn the shires were sub-divided into 'hundreds' or 'wapentakes' in the 10th century (in about 950 by Edred, son of Edward the Elder). The hundreds were further sub-divided into the manors situated within them. Bradford lies in the Black Torrington Hundred

For his enquiry William divided the country into circuits and the western circuit comprised the counties of Wiltshire, Dorset, Somerset, Devon and Cornwall. Each shire had its sheriff, the king's deputy, and for Devon this was Baldwin fitzherbert de Meuilles, son of Gilbert, Count of Brionne. He was also lord (held the honour) of Okehampton, and was rewarded by the king with many manors, among them

Bradefort, which had been held in the time of Edward the Confessor (1065) by the Saxon, Algar the tall. Here there were five tenant farmers (known as *villeins*), two cottagers (*bordars*) and six slaves (*serfs*). There were 9 cattle, 50 sheep, 16 goats and 6 pigs, and there were 30 acres of pasture, 12 acres of meadow (common land for hay-making) and 60 acres of woodland.

Besides the manor of *Bradefort* (or *Bradeford*) there were three sub-manors which were recorded in the Domesday Book: *Doneslanda* (Dunsland), *Lachebroc* (Lashbrook) and *Engestecota* (Henscott), and Baldwin was given the first two of these but they were held by under-tenants. Dunsland was tenanted by Cadio, having in Saxon times been held by Wulfric. Here there were 20 acres of pasture, 4 acres of woodland, and a similar amount of meadow, with six villeins, four bordars and one serf. There were 15 cattle. Lashbrook (formerly also held by Algar) was tenanted by Roger de Meuilles, with fifty acres each of pasture and meadow and fifteen acres of woodland. There were ten villeins, six bordars and ten serfs, 17 cattle, 45 sheep and 21 goats.

Henscott was held by Geoffrey de Mowbray, bishop of Coutances, with Drogo as his sub-tenant. It was formerly held by three Saxon thanes (Gola, Hedric and Godric). There were only two furlongs of pasture, 10 acres of meadow and 60 acres of woodland, with 20 cattle, 60 sheep and 20 goats There were two villeins and four serfs.

This would make a population in the present parish area of between 150 and 200 people. Bradford manor was valued at 40 shillings, Lashbrook at 50 shillings, Dunsland at 25 shillings and Henscott at 15 shillings. The four manors accounted for 330 acres, just under one tenth of the land which made up the parish of Bradford. The other 3,000 acres would be waste or forest where the king had rights of hunting.

All Saints Church in the 1920s: view from the East end

2

DOMESDAY MANORS

Bradford

Bradford Manor had its manor house probably near the church, though we can assume that Baldwin did not live there. His chief seat was Okehampton castle. Nothing further is documented for a hundred years until in 1166 the manor of Bradford was held by Engelram de Abernu. This name devolved into de Aubernon and then to Daubernon. Hence the manor became known as Bradford Daubernon to distinguish it from other Bradfords such as the Domesday manor of Bradford in Pyworthy (south of Bridgerule) and the manor of Bradford Tracey near Witheridge. William Daubernon held the manor in 1241 and he was succeeded by John who died in 1295. His daughter Joan married John de Deneys of Gidcot in 1285. Thus it passed to the Dennys family who were also established at Holcombe Burnell near Exeter (there was a notable family of Dennis in Pancrasweek in the second half of the 12th century). After four or five generations at Bradford, Redegund, the daughter of Gilbert Denys, married Robert Gifford of Yeo in Alwington (circa 1450) and brought the manor to that family in the late 15th century.

After another three generations it came to the Cary family through the marriage of Wilmot Gifford to her second husband Sir George Cary of Cockington. George's younger brother Robert lived at Bradford and was buried here in 1610. Sir George was Lord Deputy of Ireland in 1599, and died in 1615. None of his three children had heirs and Robert's nephew, Edward Cary succeeded to the manor. The Cockington estate was sold after the Civil war in 1654. In 1662 another Sir George Cary, grandson of Robert of Bradford, bought Tor Abbey.

The Carys reputedly came from St Giles in the Heath in the 13th century. One branch of the family inherited Clovelly in the 14th century where they continued until 1724 when it passed to Hamlyn. It can be presumed that Carys lived in Bradford at the old manor house near the church for about 50 years until the 1630s. Gradually the house became ruinous and the manor estate was sold to Thomas Grylls and John Borlase of Helston in 1809.

Dunsland

The family of Cadio held the sub-manor of Dunsland for nearly four centuries. There is a legend that Cadio murdered the former Saxon thane in order to possess the land. This resulted in a haunting of the well, which is still in existence, near the site of the old house.

Cadio (*Cadiho* or even *Cade*) continued to hold the manor until Thomasin, daughter and heir of John Cadiho, married John Dabernon, who was descended from a younger branch of the Dabernons of Bradford manor.

His father, also John Dabernon, was a lawyer and member of the Stannary Court and was member of Parliament for Devon in 1356. In 1414 Bishop Stafford granted a dispensation for the marriage of John Dabernon and *Thomacia* daughter of John Cadio because, although John knew they were related in the 4th degree of consanquinity, *Thomesyne* did not; but John was not to marry again if she died. In 1425 Alice, the widow of John *Cade*, granted unto John Dabernon and Thomazin his wife, and to their heirs, all lands and tenements in Dunsland, Cookbury, Thornbury Mill, Henscott, Westcott, Wodecot, Hole, Middlescote, Thorne and Pilton. Thomas Westcote, writing in the 1630s, records that there was a monument in Bradford church to John Dabernon of Dunsland who died in 1432.

Dunsland House in 1947.

A son, or grandson, of John Dabernon married Isabel daughter of John Mules and a daughter of this marriage married John Battin, son of William Battin of Exeter. So Battin succeeded to Dunsland. There followed three male descents - Robert, Robert and Humphry – until Philippa, daughter of Humphry and Katerin Battyn married John Arscott of Arscott in Holsworthy. Humphry Battyn died in 1522 and thus Dunsland passed to the Arscotts who were succeeded by the Bickfords in 1662. Then followed the Cohams and finally the Dickinsons, who sold the estate in 1947.

Henscott

Very little is known about the Norman Drogo. The first time the name Henscott appears as the name of the owner is in the 13th century, during the reign of Henry III, when Wilfred (or *Galfride*) de Henscot is named, who was believed to be descended from Cornu. Roger Cornu held Thornbury manor in 1132.

Richard de *Heynstecote* contributed to the Lay Subsidy assessment for Bradford in 1332 the sum of twelve pence, and the sum of nine pence was charged on Reginald de Heynstecote. At the same time both John Deneys of Bradford and John Cadie of Dunsland were assessed at 36 pence (3 shillings). The Hengescote family continued at Henscot until the 16th century. Westcote records a tombstone in Bradford church which read, 'Pray for the soul of John Hengescot esq. who deceased 30th June 1500, on whose soul Jesus have mercy'. There still remains a slab on the nave floor which reads '*Pray for the soule of John Hengiscot esquire whyche decessyth the 13th day of December in the year of owre Lorde God 1572*'. The heirs of this John were Mary, who married Sir Nicholas Prideaux, and Elizabeth, who married Thomas Pomeroy of Ingsdon in Ilsington, south Devon in 1575. There is a memorial in the church to Elizabeth who died 9th day of June 1599.

Grace English who grew up at Bradford Manor and spent most of the war years there, made an extensive research into local history. She wrote a poem about the gravestone in Bradford church:

Pray for your soul, John Henscot, do you ask?
You, forgotten for twice two hundred years.
But when you died, completed your earthly task,
You surely had your share of prayers and tears.

Tears or prayers, which lacked you most in life?
I cannot give you tears, poor lonely ghost,
I who am young, and my own time's strife
Needs many prayers to balance bright faith lost.

We with the hungry centuries between,
Whose hearts perchance have beat to the same desires,
Loves, hopes: whose wondering eyes have seen
Athwart the hills the same clear sunset fires.

Among the same green pasturelands have we,
Two questing, native spirits gone our ways,
Loved the same things with passion strong and free
And loved the earth in the fullness of our days.

John Henscot of Henscot, I who in your place do tread
And living read your mute and trusting plea,
Call from eternal Peace, you unknown dead,
A blessing on you, and ask your own for me.

At some time the manor passed to the family of Ridgeway who became the Earls of Londonderry and thence, by the 19th century, to Earl Stanhope of Chivering, who was also lord of the manor of Holsworthy. Lady Hestor Stanhope, a famous traveller who settled in the Levant in 1810, was the sister of the 4th earl, while the 5th earl was a notable historian. The title became extinct in the 1960s. Henscott was purchased by the Trible family in 1914.

Lashbrook
The sub-manor of Lashbrook held by Roger de Meuille in 1086, when it appeared to be the largest hamlet, did not expand like the other manors. It possibly never had, or soon lost, a manor house, although the name of the early lord was perpetuated by the manor retaining the name 'Moyles

Lashbrook'. John de Molis held Lashbrook together with Exbourne and Highampton in 1285. Then came Robert de Moelys, followed by James le Mulys in 1339, and another John in 1350. Thomas Prous of Exbourne appears to have held *Lachebrok* in 1411. There was a John Pruste paying tax in Bradford in 1581. At some time before the 18th century it was acquired by the Coham family of Black Torrington, and later of Dunsland.

Braundsworthy Bridge: Bradford parish boundary with Black Torrington, facing Lashbrook Wood.   (photo: D. Curno)

Middlecott

Midelcota appears several times in the Domesday Book and it is not always clear as to which is which in today's geography. If Middlecott in Bradford, which includes Kenneland, is a Domesday sub-manor then it was at the time of the conquest an outlier of Black Torrington, held by Ranulf from Baldwin. As the parochial system developed it continued to be a detached part of Black Torrington, known as the Western Hamlet, until it was included in Bradford for civil purposes in 1884. It did not become part of the ecclesiastical parish until 1929.

3

THE MEDIAEVAL CHURCH and PEOPLE

The Domesday Book rarely mentions the churches in the different manors, although it is probable that there was a Saxon church at Bradford, there is no evidence or record of any church existing before Norman times. The oval font and the arch of the south door are Norman remains. The oval fluted bowl of the font is in the Romanesque style of the mid twelfth century; originally made of local stone, the shaft has been lengthened in the course of time. The south doorway is arched with a single order of colonnettes.

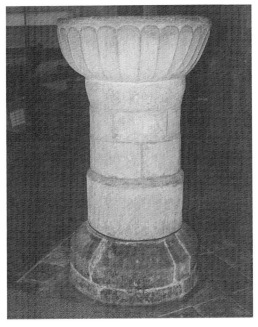

12th century font in Bradford Church.
(photo: Alan Barnes)

Added to this lack of evidence, early records of clergy and their appointments are patchy, and although we can say for certain that there was a church here in the 12th century, it is not until the 14th century that the dedication of the church (All Saints) is known. In the Episcopal register of Bishop Stapledon it is recorded that William Mewy, who was rector of Bradford, was given licence on 14th July 1309 for non-residence for a year from Michaelmas, to study in theology or in canon law. He had been ordained deacon the previous February at St German's and was priested on 15th March in the same year.

The next priest in the records is named as either William Basset (by Dr George Oliver, a 19th century historian) or William Russel (Bishop Grandisson's transcripts). George Oliver noted that William Basset was admitted to the rectory of Bradford on 18th November 1321, when the patron of the living was the Lord of the Manor, *Johannis* Deneys. Grandisson's register states that William Russel was 'Parson of Bradford' in September 1328 when he was £20 in debt and the benefice was sequestrated. His name appears again the following January as the 'Rector of *Bradeforde*'.

The next rector named is Hugh de Grettone who succeeded to the living on 12th November 1335, followed by John Sampson who was instituted on 2nd April 1349. He was inducted by Henry Cornu, rector of Thornbury, acting for the Archdeacon of Totnes. The patron for both of these was John Denys. Next came John Knyght from Whymple by Exeter, in July 1354. The following year he was granted a licence for absence, but neither the reason nor the length of time were specified. One rector in this century appears to have stayed for nearly fifty years: Roger Langle was instituted in 1363 and died in office. His successor was John Pennels, LL.B., appointed in 1412 by Isolda, widow of John Denys. The first mention of the dedication of the church to All Saints is recorded in 1373.

It is in the 14th century that parts of the present church were built: the south wall and windows of the chancel and, in this century, the east window was probably renewed and the north aisle added, although the windows in the north aisle are in the perpendicular style of the 15th century. The granite arcades separating the aisles are also thought to date from the 1430s. The tower was probably built earlier, certainly the west door and the west window are 14th century. There is a suggestion that the tower was struck by lightning about 1550 and restored and raised in height in that year, when Thomas Browne was rector. There is a date carved indistinctly in the stone near the base of the tower, by the west door, which could be read as 1550.

Apart from the clergy in the mediaeval period, for which there is an almost continuous list from 1309, there are very few others names recorded beyond those of the manors. So that besides Deneys, Cade and Heynestecote there are only another eight names which are in the Lay Subsidy list for 1332. These are John Floyer, Thomas Frauncys, Robert Mareschal, William Carpenter, John Hywyn, Martin de Clauyle, William Fullonere and William de Ryghtodan.

Place names found in mediaeval records are *Rythtedon* (*Est* and West) and *Baddeston* (Bason), in 1244, *Stodesdon* (Stadson) in 1249 and *Kytehele* (Kithill) in 1284, In the 14th century we can find *Kenelonda* (1330), *Midelcote* (1333) and *Prestecote* (1352). *Flayers* is recorded in 1462, probably the home of the Floyer family who are named in 1332. *Bovycott* does not appear before 1542, and *Hestede* (Highstead) not until 1620, with Holemore in 1623.

In Black Torrington *Brendesworth* (Braundsworthy), which possibly gives its name to the Braund family, who lived at Keneland, is mentioned in 1238.

4

TUDOR BRADFORD

By the sixteenth century we know many names of Bradford people, largely because of church records of baptisms, marriages and burials which have survived from 1558. In that year Phillippe, daughter of William Squier was baptized on 12th November, probably by Simon Atkyn who was a Doctor of Divinity and Professor of Sacred Theology. He was rector of Bradford from 1557 until his death in 1560. He had been rector of Little Petherick, near Padstow, from 1544 for ten years. William Squier was buried 7th February 1593/4. His will was proved later in that year but was unfortunately one of the many wills which were destroyed in the blitz of Exeter in 1942.

Previous to Simon Atkyn the rector was John Arscott, who was probably a nephew of John Arscott of Arscott in Holsworthy who married Phillippa Battyn, the heiress of Dunsland which she inherited on the death of her father, Humphry Battin, in 1522.

The Arscott pedigree is a difficult one to follow as there is some disagreement among the early genealogists both as to names and sequence. There were two Arscott priests in the early 16th century. Alnethius Arscott was rector of Ashwater from 1505 – 1518, and of Cheriton Fitzpaine until his death in 1537; his brother, John Arscott, being rector of High Bickington from 1514 until 1526, and of Holsworthy together with Pyworthy from 1526 until 1537. These two brothers would appear to be the uncles of John Arscott of Dunsland, who married Phillippe Battin and was buried at Bradford on

3rd May 1563, probably in the vault beneath the chancel floor. Phillippe Arscott was buried 17th June 1587.

John of Dunsland had a younger brother, also named John, who purchased the manor of Tetcott, where the Arscotts remained until the estate was bequeathed to the Molesworths of Pencarrow after a younger John Arscott died in 1788. John and Phillippa had eight sons and several daughters. The eldest son was Humphrey who lies buried in Bradford church where there is a tombstone in the floor of the nave. The stone has been broken and parts are missing. It reads:

> 'Lord Jesus Christ have merci on us. . . here lieth body of. . . humfri Arscott. . . dunsland, Esqire. . . died the 12th dai of aprill in. . . Lord God. . . 80'.

The burial register records his burial on 14th April 1580. Humphrey also had two brothers who were priests: Nicholas who was rector of Pyworthy in 1547, and rector of Dolton in 1550; and another Alnethius (or Halnight) who was rector of Shebbear from 1573 -1616. A portrait of this Arscott survives at Coham in Black Torrington.

Portrait of Halnight Arscott, vicar of Shebbear 1573-1616.

Humphrey's eldest son was another John, who married Mary Monk, sister of General George Monk of Great Potheridge; his son Arthur substantially rebuilt Dunsland House some time before his death in 1662. He was the last of the Arscotts of Dunsland, who remained Roman Catholics until the restoration of the monarchy in 1660. Whether they paid the monthly £20 fine imposed on recusants in 1581 is not known. Arthur's daughter, Grace, married William Bickford of Plympton in 1634.

Next among the 16th century families in Bradford, besides Humphry Batyn and John Arscott already mentioned, there is John Henscott of Henscott, who died in 1572. He is named in the Devon Muster Roll of 1569, together with William Maynard (the Maynards were at Bovacott in the 17th century). Among the land owners in the 16th century was William Gerne who is listed in the Devon Subsidy Roll for 1525. John Gearne was married in Bradford church to Alice Marwood in 1580. Richard Gearne was taxed on land in 1624 and Robert Gearne was churchwarden in 1712, but the name does not appear in the parish registers after 1740.

The other substantial landowner recorded in the 1569 Muster Roll is Elizabeth Fortescue. Which land she owned is unclear; it was possibly Bradford Manor through connection with the Gifford family. There is a memorial slab in the church which is only partly legible but would appear to be to

> Elizabeth forta— — late wife of Ny— — fortaschu Essqu..
> who decesyd in the ... of our Lord 1573.

But there is no entry in the burial register.

Richard Cavell (possibly a descendent of de Clauyle) was one of the wealthier parishioners named in the Subsidy Roll of 1525. He was buried at Bradford on 11th December 1560 and his widow Thomasine was buried on *Corpus Christi* day, 1562. She made a will on 26th May of that year, extracts of which have been preserved. She left to the churchwardens of Bradford 6 shillings and 8 pence for the maintenance of the church, and also one chalice. To her kinsman Alnet Browne she left £10 and also £10 to his sister Anstice, who married

William Way in 1565. To Honor, the daughter of John Browne of Bason she left £1 to be paid on her marriage. She left to her godsons, John Speccott and Thomas *Ascotte* £1 each. Thomas was probably the younger brother of John the first Arscott of Dunsland. She left to Richard Shere, the parson of Thornbury, £1 and also to John Colwell, of Bason, 6 shillings and 8 pence.

Thomasine left to her son William Cavell her best feather bed and her salt of silver 'so long as he dwell upon his benefice of Bradford' otherwise it was to go to Alnett Browne. To her son John she left her second best bed, 'and if he died without issue it was to go to Thomas White his nephew'. She left to Mr. John Arscott, Mr. William ffortescue and Mr. Richard Shere £40 'which Mr. Robert Cary of Clovelly oweth me to be paid to the children of my son Humphrey Cavell'.

William Cavell was a Fellow of New College, Oxford from 1546-53. He was granted his M.A. in 1556 and appointed rector of Bradford in 1560. He was made a prebend of Exeter in 1562 and rector of Holsworthy about 1579. He married Phillip Erisye in 1570 and a daughter, Ibbott, was baptized in January 1571/2. He was buried at Bradford on 12th January 1590/1.

Another family which is prominent in the 16th century and continues into the 1680s is Colwell. Stephen *Colwyll* is listed in 1525 as having a substantial income. In 1582 John son of Stephen Collwell of *Pristacote* was baptized, and in 1600 Ibbott, a daughter of Richard Collwell of *Pristacote* was baptized. There were two John Colwills (father and son) living at East Rightadon and *Myddell* Rightadon in the early 1600s. In 1569 there was a John Colwill living at Bason, who, together with Robert Colwill and the widow Joan Colwill, was among the wealthier residents.

In the middle of the 16th century the name Maynard appears. William Maynard presented the 1569 Muster Roll and a widow, Thomasina Maynard, appears in the 1581 Muster Roll as a land owner. The land is almost certainly Bovacott where the Maynard family continued until the beginning of the 18th century. Their son William, whose name appears in the 1624 Subsidy Roll together with Christopher Maynard (who married Frances Rawlye of Buckland Filleigh in 1613) as possessing taxable lands, had a son John who was the father of William, John, Ezekiel and Arthur.

William and Ezekiel both went up to Oxford, and William was rector of Thornbury from 1681 – 1719. Arthur died in infancy and Ezekiel at the age of 25 years. Memorials to the family can be found at the west end of the north aisle of Bradford church. John married but no male heirs survived him. He was buried at Bradford in June 1721.

Lana Cross.

5

CIVIL STRIFE

The 15th and 16th centuries were times of great change and associated dissension, both in religious understanding and in political practice. With the Reformation the supremacy of the Roman Catholic Church in Europe and much of the teaching of the Church was being questioned. The invention of printing had facilitated the dissemination of ideas.. This period also saw the rise of nationalism and the challenge of the autocratic powers of monarchies.

In 1534 the Church of England separated from the Roman Catholic Church. Two years later all small monasteries were suppressed, and by 1539 most of the rest were closed, either voluntarily or by compulsion. Thomas Cromwell issued injunctions forbidding images in churches and ordering the removal of 'superstitious' shrines. Many churches were despoiled of their ornaments and of much else besides. In 1549 the Latin mass was replaced by the English prayer book. The Prayer Book Rebellion, which began in Cornwall, swept up through Devon to the outskirts of Exeter before it was suppressed by the army sent by Henry VIII. Then there was a reversal with the accession of Mary in 1553, and change again when she died five years later. Under Queen Elizabeth a compromise was effected between the extremes of Roman Catholicism and the 'protestantism' of the ardent puritans.

In Bradford no evidence appears of any great upheaval. Thomas Browne was rector throughout the first period of this change, from 1528-1552, but there are no records of any removals (or anything else) at this time. There was a mediaeval wooden rood screen and oak benches with carved ends which survived until the 18th century. The slate altar stone, with incised crosses, may have been thrown down and

Mediaeval altar slab in Bradford Church, restored in 1881
(photo: Alan Barnes)

replaced with a simple communion table. This slate slab was discovered under the church floor in the 19th century, and reinstated within a wooden frame as part of the present altar. Thomas Browne was appointed rector of Clovelly in 1554 but was deprived of the living in 1558, for reasons now unknown. The rector who followed William Cavell (1560-1591), George Closse, was also rector of Black Torrington. In 1615 he was degraded and deprived of both livings. This was probably because of his extreme puritanism. There was a small cell of puritan clergy active in North Devon in the later years of Elizabeth's reign.

In 1624 the principal landed families are given as Arthur Arscott at Dunsland, William Maynard at Bovacott and Richard Gearne. Robert and John Colwill are among those taxed on their wealth.

In May 1641 Parliament published a 'Form of Protestation' which was sent to every town and village in the land to be signed as a protestation of dissatisfaction with the king and the Church for attempting to subvert the true reformed Protestant religion, and declaring a desire to uphold 'the Powers and Privileges of Parliament and the Lawful Rights of the Subjects'. The Protestation was read in parish churches at the end of service and all males over the age of 18 were expected to sign. It was signed in Bradford by the rector, Thomas Saltern and Robert Jeffrey, the churchwarden, and sixty four others. Christopher Colwill was declared to be bedridden and incapable, and William Paddon was deaf and unable to hear the minister's words. William Bickford is entitled 'gentleman'. Other prominent names are John Arscott, William Maynard, John Leach, Jonathan Squeire and Richard Gearne, the constable.

The English civil war, 1642-1647, raged up and down through Devon and Cornwall. The larger towns were mainly in support of Parliament, and the country landowners mainly for the king. The Parliamentarians were suspicious of the high church bishops like William Laud and of the fact that the queen, Henrietta, was a Roman Catholic. At the end of the war and with the establishment of the Commonwealth the established Church was suspended. A Directory of Worship replaced the Book of Common Prayer and many clergy with high church views were deprived of their livings and were replaced by non-conforming ministers. This happened at Buckland Filleigh where the Rector, Henry Wilson, who was chaplain to Sir Bevil Grenville at the battle of Stamford Hill at Stratton near Bude in 1643, was ejected from the living by the Parliamentarians and went to Bideford where he kept a small school. It is probable that this also happened at Thornbury but none of the old registers of that parish before 1652 have survived; and although the new rector in that year had the support of the patron we do not know what happened to his predecessor. No such thing happened at Bradford. Thomas Saltern had been rector from 1615 until he died in 1652. It is not certain whether his successor was appointed immediately, but John Tooker was in office in 1657. He had seven children by his first wife Joane baptized between 1658 and 1670. He married Jane Pengelly after the death of his first wife and they had one son baptized in 1683. The Revd. Mr. John Tooker died in August 1699. In 1849 there still remained a monument to him in the chancel floor which read 'body of the late Revd. John Tooker (died) Aug. 20 1699'. The stone also bore the arms of the Tooker family, so that we may presume that one of his ancestors was William Tooker, Archdeacon of Barnstaple in 1585, and later Dean of Lichfield, who was buried in Salisbury cathedral in 1620.

Most of the local landed families in this part of Devon seemed not to want to get involved in the conflict and tried to remain neutral. The Bampfields on the whole supported Parliament. Some families were divided, like the Fortescues, who in south Devon were for the king, and in the north (including John Fortescue at Buckland Filleigh) for Parliament. Sir Samuel Rolle of Petrockstowe was also a Parliamentarian. There was very little conflict reported anywhere near Bradford. There was a skirmish on Hatherleigh Moor in 1644 and of course the battle at Stratton. There was a legend that Buckland manor house was besieged by royalist forces, but no evidence supports the tale. There was a battle at Great Torrington towards the end of the war when the parish church was badly damaged.

6

INTO THE 18TH CENTURY

By the year seventeen hundred we can see the pattern of estates which was to last for nearly two hundred years. There were four major landowners who owned over 80% of the parish.

First there was the old manor estate, owned by the Carys of Tor Abbey who were absent landlords. This covered about six hundred acres mostly around the church and the old manor house, with West Bradford, Bason, Bradford Mill, Lana and Priestacott. Secondly, and twice as large an area, was Dunsland Manor. This included Holemoor and the lands going down to Dipper Mill bridge, Lashbrook and land stretching south from the house to Brandis Corner and New Buildings. Thirdly was Henscot, some four hundred acres, and lastly Bovacott which included Flares and Goosemoor and perhaps part of Rightadon.

The old Manor House near the church had been vacant for fifty years or more. There are no records of any Carys living in Bradford after Sir Edward Cary in the 1630s, although George Cary esq. paid a rate on a tenement in Bradford Town in 1746. It is believed that the old manor house burnt down in the 1770s.

Dunsland House however was flourishing. Parts of the house built by the Battyns in the 1550s remained, also part of the house rebuilt by the second John Arscott in 1609. His son, Arthur, died in 1662. Arthur's daughter Grace, who became the heiress, had married William Bickford from Plympton in 1634. A memorial was erected to William and Grace Bickford and is on the north wall of the church aisle with the Bickford crest surmounting it. It also commemorates Arthur Arscott.

Drawing room at Dunsland House, early 19th century painting (compare with page 67)

On Arthur's death Arscott Bickford, the son of William and Grace, set about adding a new and larger wing and, when this was completed, the grand and imposing house remained until it was destroyed by fire in 1967. Richard Polwhele described it in about 1800 as 'a garden in the wilderness' and said that the hall and suite of rooms were 'superior in design and execution to those of most houses of the same age'.

Arscott Bickford married three times. He had a daughter, Honor, by his second wife who was Honor Prideaux. After her death in 1677 he married, thirdly, her cousin Bridget Prideaux of Padstow, by whom he had seven children (four of them dying in infancy). Through the Prideaux family their descendents can trace their ancestry, via the Lutterels and the Courtenays, to King Edward I! Their eldest surviving son, William, was living at Dunsland House in 1700. He was Sheriff for Devon in 1720. It is interesting to read in the Poor Rate charges for 1695 that Mrs Bridgett Bickford pays over £6 (Arscott died in 1693). The next highest charge is £2. 1s. for

John Rigsby (probably for Flares). John Rigsby, gent, was buried in July 1726: there used to be a floor monument to him in the chancel. The Rector, John Tooker and Joakim Heysett (probably of Bovacott) paid £1. 8s. The compulsory Poor Rate was abolished in 1868.

William Bickford also had three marriages. He had five children by his second wife, Damaris Hoblyn (two of them dying in infancy; one of whom, Edward, has a memorial on the north wall of the church) and two sons by his third marriage to Elizabeth Richards. His eldest son, another Arscott, was Sheriff for Devon in 1759/60. Arscott died unmarried in 1771 and his younger half-brother, George, succeeded him. George, who married Mary Palfreyman, was a qualified surgeon and a local magistrate.

The surviving Rate Books show that George Bickford was diligent in ensuring that the Overseers of the Poor were efficient in their duties. Figures available for the period at the end of his life report that about twenty people were receiving poor relief each year. With a rising population the number increased to about 50 a year (16% of the population) in the early nineteenth century. Relief was most usually given in the form of cloth or clothing, and sometimes tools for work; occasionally as fuel (wood or furze), or food. Relief also took the form of housing for homeless children, nursing for the sick, and for sending for the doctor from Holsworthy. Financial relief might amount to 1 shilling and 6 pence a week. Agricultural wages were at this time seven shillings a week.

George's younger daughter, Elizabeth, who was baptized at Cookbury on 10th October 1773 and died in 1820, bequeathed £450 to be invested for the benefit of the poor of the parishes of Bradford and Cookbury. Owing to lack of re-investment the capital dwindled so that in 1999 the charity was officially closed and the balance of £315 was distributed among claimants from those on State Benefit in the two parishes. Henscott seems to have had several tenants during the 18th century, but the only hint of ownership is in a reference to Lord Londonderry (Thomas Pitt, Earl of Londonderry) in 1750, when he paid rates on part of Henscott.

Principal freeholders in Bradford in 1762 are Arscott Bickford of Dunsland, Lewis Heysett of Bovacott, Thomas Jeffery of Kennerland, Samuel Ley at West Rightadon and William Andrew.

There is no mention of Bovacott before the mid 16th century (1542 *Bovycott*) when it was the home of the Maynard family. In 1665 Joakim *Hessett* married Jullian the daughter of Stephen Coham, and in 1674 Joakim *Hyssed* married Sarah Collwell, and in 1680 they had a son John baptized. It seems probable that the Heysetts, who were of Black Torrington descent, occupied part of Bovacott while John Maynard was still in residence. In 1712 John Coham, younger brother of Stephen Coham of Coham, married Margaret Holland of Upcott in Sheepwash, and soon afterwards they came to live at Bovacott. Their grandson Arthur married Ruth Heysett at Bradford church in 1791. Early in the nineteenth century the entire property passed to the Heysetts and John Heysett rebuilt the house in 1810. The family continued to live there until 1876.

At the end of the lane leading down to the main road from Bovacott there used to be a large oak tree, several hundred years old and of a great girth. Kelly's Directory for 1902 states that the 'celebrated "Crooked Oak", a well-known venue for the meet of foxhounds, is supposed to be over 800 years old and has the reputation of being haunted'. It gave its name to a cottage on the Bovacott estate. The tree however is no longer there. By 1950 it had fallen and all remains of it have now vanished. One story is that the haunting is by a hunter who was caught by the neck when riding under the tree and hanged. Another is that it was haunted by the sound of a horse trotting. In 1904 the Tetcott Otterhounds were re-established with kennels on the Bovacott estate. The first Master was Mr. C. Morley Saunders of Bovacott. From 1908-11 Mr. W. H. Wyley of Beara Court in Black Torrington was the Master, with the kennels continuing at Bovacott.

In 1704 John Silke was instituted as Rector. His father, Thomas Silke, had been Rector of North Molton where he died in 1704. His younger brother, James, became Rector of Buckland Filleigh in 1717, and his youngest brother, Angel,

Morley Saunders with the Tetcott Otter Hounds on the lawn at Bovacott 1904 with his wife on the left and his son (either Leslie or Francis)

was Vicar of Sonning in Berkshire. Two of James' children married Cohams. The Revd. Holland Coham married Christian Silke in 1750 when James Silke resigned the living of Northlew, which he held in plurality with Buckland Filleigh, so that his son-in-law could take his place. Christian's brother, John, married Susanna Coham in 1751. John Silke of Bradford married Anne Cholwich and had one son, John, born in 1714, who graduated at Oxford and became Rector of Inwardleigh.

Gregory Tamblyn was instituted as Rector of Bradford in 1741 and remained in office until he died, at the age of 83, in 1799. He was presented to the living by William Bampfield of Beer, who had recently purchased the patronage from George Cary and endowed it to provide education and preferment for members of the Bampfield family. As no Bampfield was qualified for the appointment, Gregory, who was a cousin of William Bampfield, was given the living. In 1744 he reported that he held Divine Service twice on Sunday, with sermon in the morning. He also held divine service on 30th January (the day of the Martyrdom of the Blessed King Charles the First), 29th May (the Restitution of the King and Royal Family in 1660), 5th November (the Deliverance of King James I and Parliament from Massacre by Gunpowder), Ash Wednesday and Good Friday, and on Saints Days if there was a congregation. The Sacrament of Holy Communion was held six times a year: Christmas and the Sunday after, Easter and the Sunday after, Whitsun and Michaelmas. Out of 112 communicants in the parish he expected about thirty on these occasions.

At the Visitation in 1764 Mr. Tamblyn reported that he also served Sutcombe Church. There were 32 families in Bradford parish. There was no school, no chapel and no papists. In the Visitation return for 1779 Thornbury replaced Sutcombe, with Divine Service in each parish once every Sunday. He had 40 communicants at Christmas and Easter, with 20 to 30 at Whitsun and Michaelmas. By 1798 he only served Bradford with two services on Sunday, but only one in the winter because of his age (82 years). He and his wife, Hannah, had six children baptized between 1744 and 1751. Two sons died in infancy. A son, Bampfield, married Mary Sommers in 1774. They were living in Sheepwash when their second child was born in 1784. Gregory Tamblyn died in 1799 and was buried within the communion rails on the north side of the sanctuary. Hannah Tamlyn died in 1754, but her age was not recorded.

The names of the churchwardens from 1701 are recorded in the rate book of the Overseers of the Poor beginning with Stephen Jeffery followed by Elias Leach (see appendix 9). Edmund Collacott was warden in 1725 when he attended the Archdeacon's Visitation. He was in possession of a tenement at *Prestacott* in 1727. He and his wife Rachel had four children baptized between 1730 and 1738. He was buried in Bradford in November 1741.

Jeremiah Milles, Dean of Exeter, made a Visitation to the church in 1760. He wrote that 'There are four bells in the church. The roof is of slate. A Wake is held on Whitsun Monday. The land in the parish is clay and mostly pasture.

Some wheat, barley and oats are grown. The timber trees are mostly oak: 40-50 hogsheads of cider are made in a year – not remarkably good. The river Torridge often overflows; in it are caught trout with rod in spring and summer. Horned cattle are sent to market at Holsworthy, *Hatherly* and Torrington.' The closing years of the eighteenth century and the beginning of the nineteenth brought hardship for most of the population, following the harvest failures and corn dearth of 1799-1801. Labouring families lived largely on barley bread and potatoes with a small amount of bacon.

Communication and travel had never been easy in West Devon; most of the roads were mere track-ways and most goods were transported by packhorse. Coach travel may have developed in the 17th century in dryer and more populated parts of England, but it was the 18th century before there were regular coach services to Exeter from London, and to Plymouth and Bath, but they did not extend into west and north Devon until much later. The first coach to run between Barnstaple and Exeter was in 1796: called the Flying Stage, it advertised 'all the way in one day' if weather permitted. In the mid 18th century, and later, much road improvement was achieved by the turnpike trusts with toll roads. One such trust was set up in Okehampton in 1760 and in Barnstaple shortly after. There is an entry in the Parish Highway accounts for 1775 which refers to a turnpike road being made in that year below *Lanend*. This would be the road from Quickmill to Holemoor. On Donn's map of 1765 the roads from *Highwick* in Black Torrington and from *Depper Mill* Bridge turn up Adelaide Lane, past the rectory and then turn right up the present green lane to the church over Vinny (or Fenny) Bridge, then behind the church and the Manor, turning right and then left at Bonfire Corner to Bason. (Grace English believed that Bonfire field took its name from bonfires to celebrate the Battle of Trafalgar or the Battle of Waterloo). After Bason the road again followed the green lane which leads to Cookbury and thence to *Upcot* and Anvil Corner. Squire George Bickford did much to encourage road building. In the year 1775 the road was made between Holemoor and Brandis Corner; with work done on Flares Moor and Highstead and

Above: Above: Holemoor in the 1920s with the well to the left of the tree.

Below: Stone Cross Cottage in the 19th century, before enlargement circa 1900.

Keneland lanes. All this work appears to have cost only £18! Only Dunsland House had had a road connecting with the Hatherleigh - Holsworthy road.

The family of Venton appears in Bradford in this century; first at Highstead in 1727 and at Great and Little Bason by the end of the century (although it is known they were at Gortleigh in Sheepwash in the 17th century). John Venton married Thomazin Jeffery at Bradford Church in July 1724. Thomazin was the daughter of Steven Jeffery and was baptized in the church in December 1698. Their third son, Thomas, married Mary Andrew in 1756. John Venton was Churchwarden in 1735. Thomas Venton, yeoman of Shebbear, leased Great Bason from George Cary of Torr Abbey in 1768 for a term of 99 years. He was Churchwarden in 1775, and his son Stephen was Churchwarden in 1800. Stephen, who was his youngest son, moved to Bason from Highstead after marrying Grace, the daughter of John Arscott of Bradford Town (near the church), in November 1802. The Ventons were yeoman farmers, renting, not owning, most of their farms (they did own Highstead). The last Venton of Highstead was John, the eldest son of Stephen, who died at Highstead in November 1834 aged 31 years. His widow, who was Elizabeth Chapman of Black Torrington, married Henry Blight, a butcher in Shebbear in 1838. His younger brothers, Stephen and Arscott continued to farm at Little and Great Bason until the 1840s, when Arscott and his family moved to a small holding at Bennetts Hole until 1882. The Venton family continued to live in Black Torrington, Cookbury, Shebbear and Sheepwash in the 20th century.

There is not much indication of who the tradesmen were at this time, but the Overseers of the Poor accounts in 1711 record Lewis Hatherley, carpenter, John Tawton and John Burden, masons, and Robert Collacott, thatcher. Other families which date back to the eighteenth century include Braund, Mayne, Trick, Ward, Ley, Gilbert, Leach and Rigsby.

The name Trick appears in the parish registers soon after 1700. John *Tricke* was churchwarden in 1708 and William Trick in 1772. Samuel and John Trick paid rates for Bradford Mill, with 32 acres, at the beginning of the nineteenth century. The mill lies near the Torridge about ¼ mile downstream from where it conjoins with the river Waldon. Having its origin in mediaeval times it continued as a working water mill into the 20th century. Grace Trick, the widow of William was there in 1839 (William also had 50 acres at Lana). By 1857 the mill, which was part of the manor estate, was occupied by Richard Crocker. In 1878 the miller was Joseph Heard, followed soon after by Samuel Petherick. Richard Brimacombe was there by 1902. The mill was worked until 1918, the last miller being Sidney Sanders, who only worked the mill for a short time, although he continued farming the land. He previously lived at Stone Cross Cottage where he advertised for sale new and and second hand bicycles and accessories, and also repairs.

Quickmill (later Quick's Mill) appears as a property name in early 18th century. Elias Leach was there in 1775. It was presumably once a water mill powered by Whiteleigh Water, a stream which forms the parish boundary on the south east side of the parish and runs into the Torridge nearby at Cripple, but there is no record of it as a working mill in the last two centuries; in fact in the 1840s and '50s Grace Damerel kept a shop there.

There was presumably a third mill in the parish, because Cookbury Mill was on the Middlecott side of the stream which separates Bradford and Cookbury. It must have been a rather occasional mill because the stream, which runs from just north of Brandis Corner to the river Waldon below Henscott, does not carry very much water. It was part of the Dunsland estate and probably ceased as a working mill before the nineteenth century because there are no records of it as a mill as such.

Another family which goes back much further, at least to the 15th century is Braund. But because the Braunds lived in the Middlecott part of the parish, principally at Keneland, which was a detached part of Black Torrington Parish until 1884, the name does not appear in the church registers until the 18th century, when John Braund was churchwarden in 1718. A small-holding near the church of about 30 acres, known as Higher Living was leased successively to Christopher and William Braund by George Cary of Torr

Abbey in the mid 18th century. William Braund of Keneland was born about 1465. His two sons, John and William, were of Keneland and Middlecote Moor. His grandson Richard, of Braundsworthy in Black Torrington, married in Black Torrington in 1554. So the family spread to Hatherleigh, Tetcott, Clawton, and Shebbear; and another branch to Northlew and beyond.

Records of the Leach family go back to 1602 when Robert, the son of Richard Leach was baptized. In 1677 Elias Leach married Ruth Ward. He had a nephew named Ezekiel and the two names continue in the family into the 19th century by which time they had moved into Black Torrington, to Highweek and Ley. Elias Leach was churchwarden of Bradford in 1702 and the family was at *Statson* (later Stadson) between 1794 and 1807.

The Ward family can trace their lineage in Bradford to John and Ruth Ward in 1664. Another John Ward married Elizabeth Browne in 1707 and was at Dennises Tenement, (a small holding to the north of the church) in 1711 and at Higher Kettle (Kithill) in 1727. He was churchwarden in 1716 and in 1723. Their son, another John, was at Great Bason in 1756, and their grandson, a third John, who married Ann Venton, was at West Bradford, which he shared with John Brown. Running true to form a great grandson, who was a fourth John, continued at West Bradford for another generation. Two of the Wards, George and Stephen are settled in Middlecott in the early 19th century; at dwellings now known as Middlecott and Norwood Farms. In the 1840s George farmed 95 acres and Stephen farmed 60 acres. By the 20th century there were no direct descendants.

7

NINETEENTH CENTURY

The population of Bradford in 1801 was 350. It peaked in 1841 with 530 people in 100 dwellings. By 1851 there was a decrease which was ascribed to young persons moving into larger towns. In 1871 the population was down to 372, and this was largely due to emigration following the agricultural depression.

Among the tradesmen of the 19th century there was a thatcher, John Crocker of Fore Street. Also in Fore Street was James Lane, a watch and clock maker. There were shoemakers: John Sluman in Fore Street, and James Dawe at Priestacott, as well as the Bates and John Horrell at Holemoor. Later shoemakers were Lewis Ward at Holemoor, Stephen Ward at Middlecott and Richard Balkwill at Brandis Corner. Joseph Paige at Holemoor (where he had a shop), Richard Brook in Fore Street and Edward Wills at Highstead Inn were all tailors. There were several carpenters in the village at various times: William Babb at Lashbrook, John Short, Robert Sanders and William Bray in Fore Street, William Burnard at Flares, John How at Priestacott and, later, Arscott Short (later of Adelaide Cottage) in Fore Street, Samuel Stidwell at Brandis Corner and Samuel Sanders at Middlecott. There were also several masons: Samuel Sillifant, John Hunkin and William Heard in Fore Street, James Ley at Holemoor and William Brock at Lane End. William Longman, grocer and draper, had a shop at Holemoor for many years. Philip Horrell was a wheelwright and James Gilbert a blacksmith, both at Holemoor.

Mr Gilbert and his staff at the blacksmith's, Holemoor. (William Reed 2nd from the left)

Among the yeoman farmers not mentioned elsewhere were James Daniel at Lower Kithill, John Jeffery with 75 acres at South Kenerland, James Richard at Stadson, George Hatherley at East Rightadon, Samuel Ley at West Rightadon, John Moyse at East Rightadon and George Bailey at Middle Rightadon and Flares. James Strong was at West Bradford, Richard Smale at Flares, Matthew Arscott at Hole and William Quick at Higher Kithill.

Some time before 1800 the parish made provision for a Poor House which was built on the north side of the churchyard. In 1807 it was reported to be in need of repair and was re-thatched in 1833. It seems that it was probably no longer used after the Poor Law Act of 1834, and was incorporated by Mr. Joseph English in the new farm buildings about 1870. In 1807 Theophilus Mayne was instructed to make new stocks for the parish at a cost of 6 shillings and 5 pence. The stocks were usually kept in the church porch.

In the 19th century more work was done on main roads and on making further new ones. Sometime before 1850 a new road was made from Dunsland Cross to Halwill, as well as improvement to the main road from Hatherleigh to Holsworthy. In 1887 the annual Vestry Meeting voted that it was desirable that a bridge should be built over the stream

Above: Highstead Inn, circa 1920, with Norman Bailey and his wife Blanche in the doorway.

Below: Highstead Inn 1989

which divides Middlecott from Cookbury, 'traffic having greatly increased since the opening of the railway'.

The railway came to Bradford in 1879. Dunsland Cross Station was just in Bradford on the parish border with Ashwater where the line turned north from Halwill before turning west through Hollacombe for Holsworthy. This was an extension of the London and South Western Railway from Okehampton. The extension to Bude was not completed until 1898.The line was closed in 1966.

The Bickford Arms was almost certainly established by the eighteenth century. The earliest recorded licensee is Edward Smale: from 1822 to 1827. William White was the landlord from 1839-1846, and Thomas Hutchings in 1850. Richard Sanders was there in 1851. Thomas M. Facey held the licence from 1856-1859 and Thomas Palmer was landlord in 1878. He was followed in 1881 by Ezekiel Friend. Highstead Inn was only licensed for beer and cider. In 1840 George Hatherley was the landlord and in 1850 it was Edward Wills, who was also a tailor. It ceased to trade as licensed premises soon after this date. A licence was granted in 1731 to Grace Jury of Bradford to sell beer and cider, but there is no indication of the premises. There was another beer house in Cookbury, the New Inn near the church.

A Post Office was established at Brandis Corner in the 1850s. Thomas Bray was the first Post Master, while his wife kept a draper's shop. He was succeeded in the 1860s by William Jeffry. By 1878 Samuel Cole, from Ashwater, was Post Master. He was also a draper, grocer and a butcher! He stayed in business until the First World War. Initially there was only a secondary letter box at Dunsland Gate (Black Gate), but by 1893 there were letter boxes at Holemoor and Priestacott as well.

The Tithe Redemption records of 1843 provide a comprehensive list of landowners and tenants. The biggest land owner was Mr. Bickford Coham at Dunsland, with 1,365 acres. Next was Bradford Manor estate, which was 570 acres. It had been sold by the Carys in 1809 and now belonged to Messrs. Grylls, Vivian & Kendall (bankers of Helston). Henscott was 470 acres and Bovacott 337 acres. Stadson, 240

Above: Dunsland Cross Station 1960. (photo courtesy of The Bickford Arms)

Below: Black Gate: entrance to Dunsland House (photo by Maurice Thomas)

acres, was owned by Amelia Griffiths of Trentishoe and farmed by William Hole and his sons, James and Emanuel. The biggest tenanted farm on the Dunsland estate was New Building where John Sanders farmed 261 acres. Also part of the Dunsland estate was Lashbrook where Abraham Isaac and James Mason farmed 220 acres and 130 acres respectively, and the home farm at Dunsland, 173 acres, was held by Philip Venton. In Middlecott George and Stephen Ward farmed 150 acres. The Coham family also had a 400 acre estate in Black Torrington. The main farm at Bovacott, owned at this time by Lewis Risdon Heysett, was 153 acres farmed by John Hopper, while Henscott, owned by Earl Stanhope was tenanted by William Yeo. The Yeo family, who came in the 1830s, stayed at Henscott for eighty years. The largest holding on the Bradford Manor estate was Great Bason, 81 acres, farmed by Arscott Venton. A substantial tenant of Holland Coham was Matthew Arscott, the son of John and Grace Arscott, who farmed 82 acres at Hole Farm, and also rented Dennises Tenement and Pudners, north of the church, from the Manor estate. The rector had 70 acres of glebe land. There were listed thirty-four farms over 30 acres, but only eight of them were over 100 acres.

In 1884 Middlecott, which included Kenneland, High Parks and Holemoor, was transferred to Bradford Parish from Black Torrington, increasing the population of Bradford (which was 377 in 1881) by about 100.

Earl Stanhope sold Henscott in 1914 when the main farm was bought by Abraham Trible of Halsdon Barton in Cookbury.

8

RESTORATION OF THE CHURCH

In September 1811 a licence was given to recast the four bells in the church tower and to make five. This work was done by John Pennington of Stoke Climsland, when John Ward and Abraham Isaac were churchwardens. In 1819 repairs were begun on the fabric of the church. Work was needed on the porch roof and the south aisle wall. This was during the incumbency of John Bampfield, the first of that name to be instituted since the patronage had been acquired by that family. Mr. Bampfield was instituted on 18th March 1803 at the age of 44 years. He was rector for 39 years, dying in June 1842 at the age of 83. He was also assistant curate of Hollacombe, at least from 1821. During his incumbency there is some evidence of music and singing in the church. In 1807 new strings were bought for the church instruments, and for some years at this time Shadrach Spry, whose father (also Shadrach) was parish clerk from 1782-1801, was paid for assisting the church singers. John Davidson, in his notes on churches in 1849, says that there were raised seats for singers at the west end of the nave and the north aisle.

Mr. Bampfield reported in 1821 that there were 67 families in the parish. There were some dissenters, whose denomination was unknown, although they normally attended church. The rector also did duty at Hollacombe. The Sacrament was celebrated four times a year when there were 45-50 communicants.

The church repairs were not very effective and in the 1820s the whole roof was in need of repair while stone mullions of the windows were reported to be broken and new flooring was required. The new bells were not altogether successful and in 1831 one of them was re-cast. At a Vestry Meeting in May 1839 Samuel Sillifant agreed to put Bradford church in good and proper repair by Michaelmas for £10. Another of the bells had to be re-cast in 1847 and the bell frame had to be renewed.

By 1848 Parson Yule, who was instituted in 1843, was preparing to make alterations and improvements to the Rectory which had stood from Elizabethan times. He was himself apparently something of an architect and is credited with designing the new Market Hall in the square at Holsworthy in 1857.

About this time Mr Yule attempted to make a thorough restoration of the church. In October 1856 a Vestry Meeting was held under his chairmanship, which was attended by the churchwardens, William Yeo and Richard Trelevan, and by James Trick, John Willis, Samuel Facey, R. Daniel and R.J. Smith, and they agreed that the church was in urgent need of extensive repairs, and that they would need to borrow £100 in addition to a parish rate to cover the cost. It took a further eight years of meetings with various disagreements before

Bradford Church circa 1865, before restoration.

any work could start. One of the principal opponents was William Yeo, the tenant farmer at Henscott who, although Churchwarden, was a dissenter and was not in favour of so much money being spent and did not believe the roof to be in such a bad state as it was. Eventually, at a Vestry Meeting on 3rd September, 1864, when the rector's son, Thomas Yule, was churchwarden with Mr Yeo, a resolution was passed to raise a loan of £200. This was proposed and seconded by the two largest landowners, Mr Bickford Coham and Mr Lewis Heysett and passed by eight votes to six with three abstentions. The Rector then wrote to Earl Stanhope, the Revd. W. Bullock (the then lord of Bradford Manor) and Mr Hughes the owner of Stadson, and received their approval for the loan, thus securing the support of all the landowners. A Committee of Management was formed consisting of the Rector, Mr Coham and Mr Heysett, Thomas Yule and William Yeo (the churchwardens), and William Routley and Charles Mason, the overseers for the poor, to act on behalf of the Parish in all matters concerned with the repair and restoration of the church. On 21st September the Rector wrote to the Hon. Mark Rolle to purchase some Beer stone from the quarries in East Devon, for the repairs, and went to see Samuel Hooper the surveyor and architect in Hatherleigh. He also wrote to the Bampfield Trust about the possibility of a grant in aid of the restoration. A grant of £60 was received in January 1866. On 28th September a meeting was held at the Stanhope Arms in Holsworthy to sign a Deed of Security with the Public Works Loan Commissioners attested by Mr Arscott Coham, a Holsworthy solicitor, who was Bickford Coham's younger brother. The following day Mr. Yule went again to Hatherleigh to inspect the contracts for the preliminary work of taking down roofs and wall and storing the old materials. On 1st October notices advertising the work were posted at Holemoor and Brandis Corner and the specifications were made available at Highstead Inn.

On 5th October 1866 the committee met at the church. The only tenders received were from William Heard, mason, and from Richard Chowen, carpenter. These were accepted and were to take off the roofs and to stow in the churchyard all the slate and the ridge tiles; to remove all the ceilings and wall plaster and to take down such walls, windows and arches that may be required for the sum of £10. Mr Coham undertook to provide the scaffold poles and the committee would provide all other materials necessary. They would then rebuild the walls and arches at three shillings per arch(?); re-slate the roofs at 3/- per square yard; plaster (three coats) all the walls at four pence per yard and lath and plaster all the ceilings at 6d per yard. The carpenter was to divide off the chancel from the nave and aisle and to fix in the chancel as many rising seats as required and a temporary desk and pulpit; then to shore the pillars and arches as required; to remove the roof timbers and wall plates, all the seats and wood flooring, marking all the wood for replacement, and to remove and stow away all the window glass and the lead guttering, for the sum of £4. The work commenced the following day, and photographs were taken by Dobson of Holsworthy to record the un-restored condition.

Unfortunately these photos do not seem to have survived so we do not know whether the 15th century screen was still surviving at that date. Fulford Williams, writing in 1964, states that it was destroyed in 1867, but John Davidson, writing about the church in 1849 does not mention it. Mr Davidson describes the church in size much as it is now with nave, chancel, north aisle and south porch. He also records a projecting aisle on the south – 15 feet by 10 feet. He mentions coved ceilings and windows of various dates: two ancient, two perpendicular and the rest later. There were fragments of fine old stained glass, including images of the evangelists, and of our Lord crowned with thorns, and some coats of arms of the Yeo family. Some fragments of this ancient glass are preserved in the vestry window. He noted that in the chancel floor were memorials to the 'late Revd Mr John Tooker', 1699 and to John Arscott of Dunsland, 1623. There were modern deal pews and raised seats for the singers at the west end of the nave and the aisle. On the chancel floor, within the rails was the ancient slate altar stone with incised crosses. This was raised and inserted in an oak frame to make the new altar table during the restorations to the chancel by Robert Bampfield.

When work began in 1866 the re-usable roof slate was stored in the north east corner of the churchyard, known as 'Christeners Hall', where un-baptised infants were buried. When the memorials on the walls were taken down the Bickford crest surmounting the tablet to the memory of William Bickford fell, hitting William Heard on the head, giving him a severe cut.

When the roof, which was termed a 'cradle roof', was exposed, it was found that the oak was largely rotten and Mr Yeo admitted that he was wrong in thinking there was not much decay. Mr Hooper's estimate that one third of the timber should be available for re-use was optimistic. In addition the north and west walls of the aisle had been poorly built with earth mortar and very little lime. There were no large or long stones in the filling to bind the inner and outer faces of the wall together, and the roots of the ivy on the west wall were the size of a man's arm and were splitting the stones. So the west wall had to be taken down to its foundation, likewise the outside face of the north wall, while the inner face had to be taken down to the sills of the windows, and an entire new roof was required over the aisle. Unfortunately the transcript of John Yule's account of this work is lost after page 25. The final bill was for £286.

The work was finished in 1868 and the nave and aisle were again open for worship, but the restoration of the chancel, which Mr.Yule had promised to undertake, did not follow and it continued to be partitioned off for another 20 years until a new rector arrived.

In 1871 a stained glass window, representing our Lord carrying a lamb and on either side, Faith, carrying a cross and Hope, holding an anchor, was given by Miss Mary Coham and her brother Bickford Coham, 'to beautify God's house and Record the memory of their ancestors'. This is placed in the east window of the north aisle. Beneath it is a brass plaque naming the owners of Dunsland from John Cadiho in 1087 to William Holland Coham in 1790. In 1872 a window was given for the west end of the north aisle as a memorial to John and Mary Heysett of Bovacott, the parents of Lewis Risdon Heysett.

When Robert Lewis Bampfield (a distant cousin of John Yule) was instituted to the living in 1885, having been vicar of West Anstey from 1868 – 85, he set about ordering the restoration of the chancel. In this he was assisted by Joseph English. William White, F.S.A., of London was asked in 1886 to advise on the restoration of the roof. The small transept projecting from the south of the chancel was removed, a new east window was made by the mason William Heard (possibly the son of the earlier William). Further work was also done in the nave and it is believed that the carved heads on four of the corbels of the roof, on either side of the nave, were representations of Mr. Bickford Coham and Mr. Joseph English and their wives. The carpenter mostly involved with this restoration was Arscott Short of Adelaide Cottage, who was also the parish clerk at that time. A new harmonium was provided and the rural dean reported that it promised to be the best chancel in the Deanery. Robert Bampfield died in June 1888 before the project, which cost £800, was complete. His brother, John William Lewis Bampfield, was instituted before the end of the year. He had been a chaplain in the Royal Navy, from which he retired in 1880 at the age of 43. A stained glass window depicting the Good Shepherd was placed in the south window of the chancel in memory of his brother's 'zealous work and liberality'. The new chancel was opened in October 1889, but the new Rector died two months later on 2nd December.

In 1891 the second and fifth bells were recast by Mears and Stainbank of Whitechapel. In 1897 a new pulpit was erected in memory of Joseph English. Clervaux Saunders, who had purchased Bovacott after the death of Lewis Heysett in 1876, gave the oak screen for the tower-opening in 1899 as a memorial to his wife Eleanor who died in 1897, and the oak eagle lectern was presented by his second wife, Ruth, as his memorial after his death in 1905. A new organ was purchased in the same year, to replace the twenty year old harmonium. The lectern, together with a reredos behind the altar depicting Jesus and the disciples at Emmaus, painted by Edward

Arscott Short: carpenter, parish clerk and sexton. Died 1896.

Fellowes Prynne, was dedicated by the Bishop of Crediton on 12th March 1907. The reredos and painting cost £123 and was paid for by public subscription in memory of Mr. Saunders. In 1912, to commemorate the coronation of King George V in the previous year, a sixth bell was added to the tower. It was cast by Taylor of Loughborough and the three older bells were re-cast at same time, and all being hung in a new bell frame. This was done during the churchwardenship of Francis Saunders (the son of Clervaux) and George Taylor, of Manor Farm, whose memorial is in the church on the north wall, and who was warden for twenty five years

Adelaide Cottage.   (photo: D. Curno)

Above: Adelaide House.   (photo: D. Curno)

Below: The Rectory circa 1930

9

THREE FAMILIES.

<u>Yule</u>

John Carslake Duncan Yule was born at Colyton in east Devon. His mother was Elizabeth Carslake. He went up to Oxford University (Christ Church) in 1821, but does not appear to have graduated. John held the living of Coldridge from 1838.

The newly built manor with Church Cottage, circa 1870.

On 13th December 1842 John Yule was instituted Rector of Bradford by the newly formed Bampfield Trust which comprised of the rectors for the time being of the parishes of East Down, Bratton Fleming and Goodleigh. This Trust held the advowson until 1989 when it passed to the Diocesan Board of Patronage. John Yule's mother was the daughter of Bampfield Carslake and thus a member of the Bampfield family, enabling him to qualify for appointment by the Trust. His father was Commander John Yule, R.N. who served on H.M.S. Victory under Admiral Nelson at the Battle of Trafalgar in 1805 (when his son John was three years old). From 1843 John Yule also held the living of Hollacombe.

As has been said, in his early years at Bradford he was very busy with building and repairs. In 1848 he took out a mortgage on the glebe rents of £687 to enlarge, repair and alter the parsonage house. In 1861 he entered into a contract with Grylls and Millett, of Helston, to purchase the Bradford Manor estate for £5,781, but by 1863 he was obviously in financial difficulties as the purchase sum with interest was taken on by the Revd Walter Bullock of Essex, who then sold the estate to Joseph Thomas English. Mr English rebuilt the derelict old manor house as a farm house and leased it until it was occupied by his youngest son, Alexander, in 1915.

By 1868 Parson Yule had been declared bankrupt and Mr English related how the parson evaded the bailiffs for thirteen weeks, taking the services on Sunday when he could not be apprehended between the hours of 6 a.m. and 6 p.m. He left the Rectory by a back door concealed beneath a pile of faggots and galloped to Millhook in Cornwall, where his brother Thomas Newte Yule lived, to be safe during the week. Mr English also related that the parson used to recite the psalms from memory, and that he used the parish tithe map to cover the window of his apple loft! If this is true it survived the experience. After the formation of the Parish Council the councillors voted that it should be given into their keeping, and used to identify fields in connection with the parish rate. Unfortunately it has not survived with the parish records, although the Record Office in Exeter has a copy.

There is also a tale, told by Grace English, that John Yule invited her grandfather to dine with him at the New Inn, Bideford. He was bemused by the way the parson ate his duck – bones and all – but was less amused when he was left to pay the bill! This lack of money would account for the fact that John Yule never restored the chancel of the church as he had declared that he would.

While very capable in many ways Mr Yule was somewhat lax in entering the records of baptisms and burials. His nephew, Henry William Yule, the Rector of Shipton-on-Cherwell, filled in the burial register after his uncle's death, from notes left in his diaries. The record of many baptisms in the 1860s and 70s is lost.

John Yule married a cousin, Jane Carslake, and had three children, John Bampfield, Thomas William and Elizabeth Jane, who were all born at Clannaborough near Copplestone. His eldest son, John, was a wine merchant but died at the age of 46. His widow was left virtually penniless and with six of her seven children came to live at the Rectory with her father-in-law. Parson Yule's wife had died three years earlier in 1876; John Yule died in 1885, having been rector for 43 years. The last Yule to be buried in Bradford was John's youngest sister, Emma Agnes Judith Yule, who died in 1916 at the age of 96 years.

The last of the Bampfield family to hold the living was another distant cousin of John Yule, John McWilliams Bampfield, who was Rector from 1903 – 1911.

Coham and Dickinson

Dunsland passed to the Coham family in 1817, through the marriage of Mary Bickford with the Revd. William Holland Coham in 1790. The last Bickford was her brother Arscott, who died unmarried. The house at Coham had suffered badly from fire in the 18th century so William & Mary were able to live at Dunsland. William was born at Northlew Rectory, where his father Holland Coham was the incumbent. William became Rector of Halwill and also assistant curate of Black

Torrington but continued to live at Dunsland with his family until his death in 1825.

His eldest son, William Bickford Coham, was also a clergyman and lived at Dunsland with his family and his younger unmarried brother, Holland Coham. Holland, who was a cripple, and his elder sister Mary moved to the Towers in Charles, Plymouth, after their nephew (William Bickford's eldest son) married in 1857. The Revd. William Bickford Coham never held a living himself, but assisted his father at Black Torrington and Halwill. He continued to assist at Black Torrington and Highampton after his father's death, until he died at Dunsland in 1843.

His son, William Holland Bickford Coham (known as Bickford) who gave much assistance in the restoration of Bradford Church, continued living at Dunsland until 1878. That same year he moved to the house at Coham, where he had rebuilt the west front of the house, and where he died in 1880.

Dunsland (which was entailed in the male line) passed to his nephew Arscott Harvey Dickinson, the only son of his sister Augusta who had married Capt. Harvey George Dickinson of the Indian Army in 1858. (*see family tree in Appendix 11.*)

Within days of the wedding Capt Dickinson was recalled to India because of the Indian Mutiny. He and his wife remained there for nearly ten years during which time their son, always known as Harvey, was born. On the voyage home Major Dickinson died and on reaching England Augusta went to live with her bachelor brother, Arscott Coham, who was a solicitor in Holsworthy. When her elder brother Bickford left Dunsland the house was let to a series of tenants so that none of the family lived there for thirty four years. During the sixty years when the Coham family lived at Dunsland the estate must have reached its zenith. Ten men were employed out of doors and there were nearly as many indoor servants.

Harvey qualified as a barrister but had little success as an advocate and the only law he practised for many years was as a local Justice of the Peace at Stratton and Holsworthy. Harvey married Mary, the eldest daughter of the Revd. Sabine Baring-

Holland Coham (1807-1867)

The Reverend William Bickford Coham, died at Dunsland in 1843

Drawing room at Dunsland House circa 1870, with elaborate carving in the style of Grinling Gibbons   (photo: Henry Hayman of Launceston)

Gould, and they had three sons. Between 1904 and 1907, when Dunsland was vacant they moved from their home in Bude to Dunsland, but only stayed there three years. During the First World War Dunsland was left empty but after the war Harvey and Mary Dickinson and their youngest son, Bickford, took up residence. Ivy covered the house and the two private drives were so bad that in winter they were impassable. Bickford and his father worked hard quarrying stone and carting it to repair the drives so that by 1923 when they bought their first motor-car the roads were at least passable. Forty windows around the house had to be repainted which Bickford did all by himself. The old roofs were in a bad condition and the cost of renewing them was prohibitive, so Bickford with the local mason James Ley and his son Ernest, grouted them with liquid cement which made them water-tight.

During the Second World War a mine was dropped in a neighbouring parish which did little local damage but the blast travelled up the valley and shook Dunsland House so that a little later the roof over the library collapsed and the only repair that could be effected was by some sheets of galvanised iron. During these war years a number of evacuee mothers and children were accommodated at Dunsland. For a while the evacuee children had their schooling in the chapel schoolroom. During these years Mr and Mrs Dickinson are remembered bicycling to Holemoor to buy their groceries.

By now the house and grounds were visibly deteriorating. Mary Dickinson, crippled with rheumatism and without any domestic help in the house, died in February 1945. Harvey felt he could not carry on without her and decided to sell Dunsland: the first time in nine hundred years of recorded history. The sale took place in 1947. It is interesting to note that the house had neither electricity nor mains water supply. This applied to all but one of the properties of the estate, including New Buildings Farm, the two Kennelands and East and West Norley. The only property with mains electricity was the Bickford Arms. Dunsland house and grounds were bought by a speculator in order to sell the timber. Some of the farms were bought by their tenants.

In 1949 the house was re-sold to Mr Philip Tilden who had been asked by Devon County Planning department to survey the house which he found in a distressed condition and taking in water whenever it rained.

Mr Tilden, fearing that nothing was going to be done to remedy this situation, bought Dunsland in order to try to restore the old house himself. However, constrained by limited finances, he sadly demolished the early Tudor wing and effected only 'patchwork' restoration. He did however pay the previous purchaser £5 for each tree that he left unfelled! After he died in 1954 the house was sold to the National Trust who re-roofed the Jacobean and Restoration wings and opened the house to the public. On 17th November 1967 tragedy struck and the house was burnt to the ground. Only the eighteenth century granary remained intact. This was subsequently moved by the National Trust to their estate at Arlington Court near Barnstaple.

Above:
Mary and Harvey
Dickinson c1942

Left: Bickford
Dickinson, air-raid
Warden 1942

Above: Dr Gwynne & Katharine in the Justice room at Dunsland House in 1962.

Below: Dr Gwynne & Katharine outside Dunsland House in 1962

English

When Parson Yule defaulted on payment for the Manor Estate it was bought by the Rev. Walter Bullock who in turn sold the estate and the lordship of the Manor to Joseph English in 1868.

Joseph English's father, Thomas English, lived in Kingston upon Hull, but Joseph was in partnership with his brother in the family timber importing business and lived for many years at Stamford, and in Northamptonshire. He had four children from his first marriage, and married secondly Rachel Anne Wallis, by whom he had nine children. A younger son, Alexander (Alec), was born in Stratton in 1871, where the family lived for a few years. Joseph then moved to Honiton where he was living in 1880. Intermittently he lived at a cottage in Bradford which he named Manor Cottage, presumably so that he could survey the restoration work being carried out on the estate, which he originally bought for the timber but then became rather attached to it. In 1871 on the site of the former manor house he built a farmhouse; Bason farmhouse was also re-built about this time. The manor farm was leased to John Weaver in 1872 and to William Bright by 1880. George Taylor, who had rented Bason, moved up to the Manor Farm about 1890. George Taylor died in 1912 and his sons carried on until the lease expired in 1915, when Alexander English took possession and it became the Manor House.

Alexander served in the Indian Civil Service from 1902 – 1920. He regulated the Co-op. Credit Societies in Burma for many years, residing at Maymyo near Mandalay. He intended to retire in 1915 but because of the war was asked to stay on in Burma and from 1917-18 was Director of Recruiting. Meanwhile his wife Fanny, the daughter of Dr. John King of Stratton, whom Alec married in 1904, returned with her two daughters, Mary and Grace, to Bradford and set about adapting the farm house into a suitable Manor House. Alec finally returned to England in 1920. Grace later married Dr. Patrick Smyth, and did much to record local and family history.

Bason Farm in the year 2000.   Photo by Catherine Smale

Alexander's eldest brother, William, was an assistant master at Rugby School but died at the early age of 46 years at Bradford. His second brother, Major Joseph English, lived at Halberton, after retiring from the army. The third brother, Frederick Paul, was in the Royal Dublin Fusiliers, served in the South African War and was awarded the D.S.O. during service at the Aden boundary dispute in 1904. He rose to the rank of Brigadier General and after being made a Companion of the Order of St. Michael and St. George in 1917, he retired and moved from Marhamchurch to Sheldon Court, Dunkeswell. His fourth brother, Charles, was a Colonel in the Royal Artillery, who retired to Barn Park, Halwill, where he died in 1925, and his younger brother, Oswald, was in the Royal Navy.

Alexander had two elder sisters, Katherine, who married Dr Francis Voelcker of Marhamchurch, and Stephanie who was a Fellow of Newnham College, Cambridge. She came back to live at Priestacott House, which the English family had built in 1904, until her death in 1957.

Joseph English gave new stained glass for the west window of the church tower and after his death in 1892 his widow gave a new pulpit in his memory in 1897. He also gave land to extend the churchyard in 1887. The lower churchyard was the gift of Alec English in 1931. After Priestacott House was built Joseph's widow Rachel lived there, with her daughter Stephanie, until her death in 1920. In that year the family sold Bason Farm to John Smale who had been their tenant there since 1891. Alexander English, who was now living permanently at the manor beside the church, was Churchwarden from 1931-33, and from 1943-53. After his wife, Fanny, died in 1944 the Manor was sold to Col. Micholls and Alec lived in Church Cottage until 1953 when he went to live with his daughter Grace in Oxford where he died at the age of 90 years in 1962.

Bradford Manor, restored as a farmhouse, circa 1890

The English Family, 1943. Mary English, Grace Smyth with her three children (Tristram, Susanna, and Margaret), and Alec English.

Above: Painting of Priestacott House, from the south, circa 1912, before alteration.

Below: Priestacott Cottage from the East (before the extension built by Col. Brook-Fox in 1960). The Rectory on the right.

10

BRADFORD SCHOOL

The earliest reference to schooling in the parish is in 1790 when Elizabeth Crocker was paid 1/- a week from the poor rates for schooling the poor children. In the mid nineteenth century there is evidence of private or dame schools. Two schoolmistresses are listed in the 1851 census: Elizabeth Bailey at Bradford Town, and Maria Walter at Priestacott.

In the 1870s the leading parishioners decided that they wanted a school. They decided that it should be nondenominational, but they also wished it to be voluntary. This meant it avoided the statutory rules and regulations imposed on board schools and relied on a voluntary and not a compulsory rate. The School opened in 1878 on land given by Mr Bickford Coham of Dunsland, and the first master was William Henry Toze. He was born in 1854 in Uffculme, East Devon, and served four years at Whitgift School in Croydon before passing his final certificate exam.

Mr Toze quickly won and kept the respect of his managers and of the district. He was regularly elected chairman of the parish meetings held annually for the election of school managers, was organiser of the local flower show, church organist and secretary of the Holsworthy District Teachers Association.

The managers were elected annually at a ratepayers meeting and varied in number from nine to eleven. Voluntary rates of two pence, and later three pence, in the £, were successfully raised in the knowledge that the cost could have been greater if it were a board school with its additional expenses. The rector was usually the vice-chairman. The religious instruction policy stated:

> 'Bible read with comment, Lord's Prayer, Creed and Commandments taught.'

This evidently satisfied the large local nonconformist element. When a New Aid Grant was introduced in 1897 it was only payable through the National or British Societies. As Bradford School belonged to neither, the managers opted for the nonconformist British Society. Under the Education Act of 1902 the school was transferred to the County, and the buildings were improved. The original school was built to accommodate 120 children from the parishes of Bradford and Cookbury. The average attendance in the late 19th century was between 80 and 90. In August 1882 a case of diphtheria was reported and in February 1891 a case of scarlatina. In March 1891 the school had to be closed because of scarlet fever.

William Toze's record, as shown by inspectors' Reports, was almost consistently good. In 1883 the Rural Dean noted that

> 'I have never visited a school better conducted, or where the children were better taught.'

In that year Mr Toze wrote in the Log:

> 'In the time I have occupied this situation corporal punishment has been inflicted no more than twice a year and never on girls. It is only used for offences of lying, bad language and truant–playing. . . happily very rare.'

In 1903 the school buildings, which according to William Toze had been little better than a barn, were remodelled. Mr Toze married his wife Philippa when he came to Bradford, or shortly before. They lived at the School House where they had five children. He had good health until he developed heart trouble in 1917. In 1919 the managers hoped he would remain at the school as long as his health permitted, which he did. He completed the school Log on 25th July 1919 and died on 31st. His widow and eldest daughter moved to Southbourne on the road to Brandis Corner. Mrs Toze died in 1925, and their daughter Una in the following year.

Mr Toze was succeeded by Stanley Gilbert, a stern disciplinarian who stayed for just over ten years. He had two assistant mistresses one of whom was Mrs Blanche Bailey the wife of the local tailor, Norman Bailey of Highstead Inn, also remembered for her stern discipline. Mrs Bailey started teaching in 1906 under Mr Toze when she was Miss Blanche Barrett.

The school had been founded to educate children from 5 to 14 years from the parishes of Bradford and Cookbury. In 1948 children aged 11 years went to school in Holsworthy, but in 1952, when Thornbury School closed, the school served that parish also. The last Head Master to live in the School House was Mr Bentley, who came in the mid '60s, but shortly afterwards moved to his own house in Cookbury.

Bradford School with Mr & Mrs Toze on left in 1906

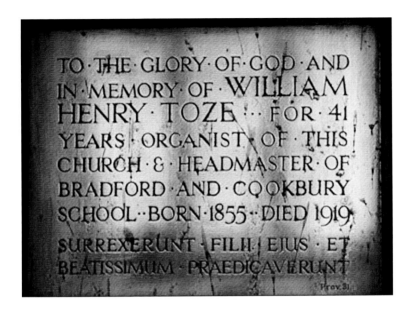

Above: Memorial to William Toze in Bradford Church.

Photograph by Alan Barnes

Below: Bradford School children with Stanley Gilbert on the right in 1930.

Bradford Primary School 2012: Head teacher Jo Dymond top left.

11

SHOPS AND TRADE.

Joseph Paige has already been mentioned as a tailor. In the 1840s he also had a draper's shop at Holemoor and expanded this to include groceries. In the 1850s Thomas Bray at the Post Office at Brandis Corner, where his wife had a draper's shop, also expanded into groceries.

William Longman started his shop at Holemoor (in the building now known as The Hole) before 1850, assisted by his son, also William, and also a tea dealer. Together they continued the business there for almost fifty years. The shop was taken on by Bethuel Hutchings in about 1895. He had come to Bradford a few years before, from Week St Mary, to farm Highstead. At the same time his brother William began to farm Hole. Bethuel Hutchings advertised, in 1910, as a *'Gents Outfitters, with suits, coats and breeches to measure'*. By 1920 the shopkeeper was William Stevens who employed two assistants. He declared himself to be a *'Draper, Grocer, Provision Merchant, Dealer in flour, meal and bran, boots and shoes, glass and china, and enamel goods'*.

He was followed in 1937 by Leslie Codd who stayed at Holemoor until 1976. The Codd family came to Holemoor in the 1920s. They were a very talented family with musical and artistic skills. Together with others in the area they formed a concert party: Mr. Codd snr. was the comic, his eldest son Arthur played the banjo, while the daughter Violet was an accomplished singer. The younger brother, Leslie was a conjurer. His brother Arthur took on Parsons Garage in

Holsworthy. He led a dance band and would come to play at dances held in the old church hall in Bradford. Leslie Codd was also churchwarden from 1970-1976.

In the 1920s and 1930s Norman Bailey had a shop at Highstead, advertising himself as *'Gentleman's Tailor and Outfitter: with a good selection of caps, ties, socks and braces; Sports coats and Flannel trousers'*. The last to run the shop at Holemoor were Messrs Mitchell and Webb but it only survived for two years, closing in 1978.

There was a butcher's shop in Holemoor from about 1890 when the Northcotts (father and son, both named Roger) opened a business in Fore Street where the younger Roger Northcott was succeeded by his son William in 1924, and he in turn by his son-in-law, Norman Southcott. When Norman Southcott retired in 1974 the shop was taken on by Charles and Rodger Broomfield (father and son) until the shop closed in 2002.

In 1910 John Hopper, who was primarily a painter and decorator, had a hardware shop in Fore Street which also sold groceries, and after he died in the early years of the Second World War his wife continued it for a while, mostly as a sweet shop.

On the other side of Holemoor, on the road leading to the school, there had long been a blacksmith's shop. James Gilbert was there in the 1840s, when it was called 'Bennetts', and George Gilbert was there at the beginning of the 20th century. After a marriage with the Reeds, William Reed, who was a Methodist lay preacher, was the blacksmith by the beginning of the First World War until he died in 1947 and then the blacksmiths shop was closed. His son Bryan had his own business in Holsworthy. There was another blacksmith shop at Brandis Corner - situated between the Bickford Arms and the Wesleyan Chapel. John Knight of Halwill was there in 1881 and Samuel Sanders, who came from Clawton, was the smith in 1900.

When Philip Horrell plied his trade as a wheelwright in the 1850s his premises were at Bennett's Hole (this designation covered the whole area between the chapel and Ivy Cottage). Hedley Hutchings (son of William) had a wheelwright's shop

Above: Butcher Northcott at Holemoor circa 1912. From left: Mrs Sillifant
& her daughter, Hilda Hopper, Roger Northcott and two others.

Below: William Reed, Emily Reed, Mary Gilbert and Rosalie Gilbert and
Mrs Fowler.

at Holemoor (opposite the blacksmiths) during the first half of the twentieth century, while his brother Harold farmed at Hole.

By the late nineteenth century threshing was increasingly done mechanically with steam engines driving the threshers and in the early twentieth century the Headdon family established their threshing business in Bradford. Owen Headdon built Southbourne in 1915 with sheds near the road to house the machinery. Richard Headdon lived at High Park and continued the business until the Second World War.

With the advent of motor vehicles Melville Daniel opened a cycle shop and garage at Brandis Corner. After the war John Cox took over the business before moving to the Post Office, where he followed Mrs Beare. She had come with her husband Fred in 1923 and continued as Post Mistress after his death. John Cox was also churchwarden from 1953–1977. After Mrs Barnard, who was Post Mistress from 1981-1987, Stanley Simpkins was the last Post Master before the Post Office was closed in March 2004. The garage at Brandis Corner continued in business, with a shop at The Laurels, until the Hillmans left in 1988. Fred and Marie Burrows continued to sell petrol until the early 1990s.

Nathaniel Heard, from Clawton, was landlord of the Bickford Arms from about 1890 and in 1906 he advertised the inn with '*spacious stabling and accommodation for motors, cyclists and pleasure parties*'. Joshua Stacey became the landlord in 1917 and stayed for thirty years. Gordon Tremaine was landlord for ten years from 1975. The Bickford Arms was thatched in the 1990s when in the ownership of Keith Phipps. As a result of a chimney fire in January 2003, when Nigel Kivell was landlord, it suffered extensive damage and was closed for re-building, and roofed in slate, until it re-opened in December 2004.

Maud Isaac set up a newsagents shop at Bickford cottage opposite the Bickford Arms in the mid 1940s, which she carried on for over forty years; selling her own hens' eggs and Jersey cream as well.

Above: William Stevens outside Holemoor grocery stores.

Below: Holemoor, 1989.

Above: Sunnyside (now Bramble Cottage) On the right Annie Balsdon with
Stanley (Frank's younger brother) 1914.

Below: Holemoor today with Roy Prowse and his forage harvester

12

PARISH COUNCIL

Parish Councils were formed as the lowest tier of local government in 1894. In Bradford a parish meeting was held in the day school on 4th December to elect seven councillors. The headmaster, Mr. Toze, was invited to chair the meeting which was attended by about 90 electors. Eighteen candidates were nominated. These were first questioned by the electors and after the election the following were declared councillors: George Gilbert, blacksmith, Samuel Cole, postmaster, William Prower Hutchings, farmer, William Bailey, farmer, William Wonnacott, farmer, Russell Rawes, rector, and George Taylor, farmer. The council held its first meeting on 13th December, 1894 and William Bailey, father of Norman, was elected chairman. The Revd. F. Russell Rawes was elected vice-chairman and clerk and Mr Bailey was also elected treasurer. Mr Matthew Yeo of Henscott was elected as District Councillor in 1895. He was chairman of the Holsworthy Rural District Council from 1900-1922.

In the first few years there were changes of membership nearly every year; only in 1901 did they adopt a three year term. In 1896 Bethuel Hutchings, shopkeeper of Hole Moor and Col. W. Bickford, R.M. (probably not related to the old Bickford family) who rented Dunsland for a few years, replaced Messrs Wonnacott and Taylor. Bethuel Hutchings was elected chairman for 1896; Russell Rawes chairman in 1897 and W. P. Hutchings of Hole chairman in 1899. George Taylor returned to the Council in 1897 when Col. Bickford left the parish. Mr Wonnacott of Stadson was re-elected in 1899, in

Above: Holemoor – looking towards Fore Street. A young Bryan Reed in the centre and Hedley Hutchings in the shadow on the right.

which year James Parsons, carpenter of Priestacott was elected. Until 1914 it was usual for between 30 and 60 electors to attend the annual meeting, but after that date never more than a dozen.

The Council agreed to hold four meetings a year which would be public, other meetings as necessary would be private. It continued some of the business of the old Vestry Meeting such as allocating the rates and appointing two over-seers from among the local farmers to assess and collect the rates. The two overseers acted individually, each taking a half year charge. At the beginning of the nineteenth century there were only twenty six ratepayers out of a population of over 300, but this number would have increased over the years. The Council took possession of the old rate books and highway accounts, the vestry minute book and, despite the Rector's objection, the tithe map and the apportionment.

Mr Toze offered to prepare the fire and light the lamps in the school for each meeting. After the initial expenses of books and of an oak chest in which to keep everything, an annual precept of £2 was made to cover council expenses. This was raised to £5 in 1928.

One of the items of business in January 1895 was the provision of allotments. There were 14 applicants. A sub-committee was formed and after much discussion they had a list of seven applicants in 1896 for various sites amounting to 14 acres. Another regular topic was footpaths and the state of the roads. Both a footpath committee and a sanitary committee were formed. In 1895 the Council requested that the County Council be responsible for the road from Brandis Corner to Dipper Mill. The main footpaths ran from Stadson to Lashbrook and from Lane End to Priestacott. The former was wet and the Water Lane part needed widening, and the latter had a bridge which frequently needed repair. The footpath from Rightadown to Goosemoor seemed to cause no trouble, but the way from Rightadown to Whiteley Meadow was discussed and the Council resolved that it was a right of way for neighbouring tenants not a public footpath and therefore no

Above: The Rectory garden circa 1914 (possibly the Revd. & Mrs John Snow) with William Curtice, the gardener.

Above: Brandis Corner looking north, the Post Office on the right.

Below: Closure of the Post Office 2005. (Cass and Maureen Simpkins).

Above: Bickford Arms circa 1900

Below: Bickford Arms after the fire in 2003

concern of the Council. The road which caused most trouble was that from Highstead Inn to Bovacott and Crooked Oak which was regularly referred to the District Council surveyor. In the 1930s, with the advent of motorised traffic the Council was concerned about dangerous corners, especially on the road from Quickmill to Priestacott and the Rectory, and at West Bradford. Most were resolved by cutting the banks back. A request was made in 1936 for the road to be widened between Middlecott Cross and Cookbury bridge especially because it was part of the route for the school bus. One of the sanitary concerns was Buddle Pond near Bennett's Hole.

As early as 1896 there was a request for a parcel office to be opened at Hole Moor. As this was not forthcoming the Council requested that the Post Office be moved from Brandis Corner to Hole Moor and continued to make this request without success for the next ten years. In 1931 the Council asked the Post Master General for a telephone box to be provided at Hole Moor: in 1934 it was approved, but the Council would have to pay £16 a year rental which was thought to be too much. The question of a street light at Hole Moor was raised in 1901 but not thought to be necessary. The Council arranged a welcome for the return of Col. Fred English from the South African War in 1902. He was to be met at Dunsland Cross station, afterwards the church bells should be rung and a thanksgiving service held.

In 1906 George Taylor of Bradford Manor Farm replaced W.P. Hutchings as chairman, but after the elections in 1907 George Gilbert of Hole Moor was elected chairman. Mr Taylor continued as a councillor until his death in 1912. In the early years of the twentieth century the Council was asked to arrange classes in technical and higher education such as sheep-shearing, dress-making, thatching, ploughing and dairy work. Some of these in the 1920s were held in the Chapel schoolroom.

Celebrations for Queen Victoria's Diamond Jubilee and King George's Silver Jubilee were passed to local committees which combined with Cookbury. The latter occasion was celebrated with a united Service in the school-room, tea, sports, a Social, bonfire and fireworks. In 1910 Miss Stephanie

Bovacott House before and after restoration.

Photograph by Maurice Thomas.

English was elected as the first woman councillor, but only served for three years, and no other woman was elected until after the Second World War. The rector, Mr McWilliams Bampfield, was elected chairman of the new council in 1910, but on leaving the parish the following year Miss English was elected in his place. W. P. Hutchings returned to the Council in 1913 and was again elected chairman. He withdrew his name from the election in 1919, when James Parsons, now of Fore Street, was elected chairman and Francis Saunders of Bovacott, who had returned from war service, was elected vice-chairman. Mr Parsons remained chairman until 1937 when William Reed of Hole Moor became chairman and continued until 1946.

The earliest minute book ends in 1940, and unfortunately the minutes for the next forty years have been lost, though there is a list of the nominations for 1946. There were only seven nominated so that Eric Heard and E.S. Isaac, both of Middlecott, Norman Bailey, Harold Hutchings, W.J. Trible, S.J. Stacey and H.J. Perkin were returned unopposed. Sometime in the late 1970s Cookbury and Bradford formed a joint parish council.

After the war the Parish Council requested the Rural District Council to build some council houses in the village. A site was identified north of Hole Moor and south of what was locally known as 'sixpenny corner'. Eight council bungalows were built in 1953 and named Queens Park to commemorate the coronation of Elizabeth II in that year.

In 1977 the Council restored the parish well at Holemoor in commemoration of the Queen's silver jubilee. In August 1995, under the chairmanship of Cass Simpkins, the Council organized a successful celebration of the 50th anniversary of VJ Day (victory over Japan). In 1997, while Roger Pole was chairman, the Council made a 'Parish Appraisal'. The results were published in June 1998 which revealed replies from 165 out of 208 properties, with overwhelming support for the village school, a new village hall and waste recycling facilities. There was a high percentage of vehicle ownership which was not surprising with the poor state of public transport. There was little support for housing development other than single units for local needs. Many felt that the roads were in bad condition and that speeding traffic was a problem. There was a marked concern for the care and planting of more trees.

An election for a new council was held in 1999. The former councillors (of the Bradford & Cookbury Council) were Roger Pole, chairman, George Griffiths, Stephen Oke, Michael Fry, Bryan Isaac, Margaret Etherington, John Trible, Freda Broan, Colin Heard, William Penn, Christopher Reed, and Graham Dart. John Gray, Andrew Oke, Robert Smale, Jenny Brown and Molly Price-Thomas were elected as new councillors, taking the places of Messrs Pole, Oke and Dart and Miss Broan, who did not stand for re-election, and of Bryan Isaac.

Winnie-the-Pooh in the old hall. Gerry Matthews as Eeyore and John Granger as Pooh

13

VILLAGE HALL

The old church room served the parish as a village hall for Bradford and Cookbury for twenty years from 1979; first under the chairmanship of Eileen Hayler and then Lorna Harris. Here were held coffee mornings, dances, jumble sales, village shows and art and craft exhibitions. The hall committee sponsored a newsletter in the late 1980s. This was first edited by Jane Francis and Mel Roe, and later by Jane until 2000, after which Martin Taylor took responsibility for two years. Then Jane and Sheila Granger edited it until 2006. In the 1980s a regular series of concerts were arranged with the help of Jane Francis, with the profits being divided between the Church, the Chapel, and the Village Hall. These concerts went under the general title of 'Spice of Life' and continued for most years until 1998, featuring songs, sketches and choruses. From 1991 Jane adapted a number of plays from popular novels, beginning with 'Death in Devon' (with Hercule 'Parrot') and ending with 'The Jungle Book' on 11th December 1999 with a cast of twenty.

In 1989 a proposal was made for a new hall with a separate skittle alley and a permanent stage. In 1997 the parish set up a Project Team under the chairmanship of Ray Radford, and an architect, John Simmons of Torrington, was appointed in November. On 20th April 1998 preliminary plans were presented at a public meeting. The site would be on land adjacent to the Primary School given by Mr Oke, and before the end of the year planning permission for the new hall was granted. In December it was announced that the National Lotteries charity had offered £243,347 towards the cost of the project. Matching grants were given by the Community Council of Devon and Torridge District Council and over £10,000 was raised locally. The new Bradford and Cookbury village Hall cost £350,000 and was officially opened on the 8th December 2000 by Torridge District Councillor Desmond Shadrick .

The old Village Hall, before its sale in 1999.

The new Village Hall in 2001.

14

SPORTING ACTIVITIES

Besides the Fox and Otter Hunts already mentioned there is little evidence of collective sporting activity. The Revd. John Powell, one time Rector of Buckland Filleigh, made copious notes about local history. Writing of the period about 1880 he describes the sport of *'outhurling'* engaged in by the parishioners of Bradford, Cookbury and Black Torrington. This took place on Whiteleigh Meadow after haymaking and apparently involved chasing a ball between certain points, rather like 'hurling', possibly with sticks as in hockey. A form survives at St Columb Major on Shrove Tuesday. Play would last for several hours and many of the players would fall out before the end of the day. The gentry would often ride out to watch. Powell mentions parsons John Yule, and John Russell of Black Torrington, as well as squire George Coham of Sheepwash. The champion of the day was Tom Shadwell, 'a man of stalwart frame and muscular limbs' (he was probably one of the Stidwill family who were carpenters in Cookbury). John Powell wrote that

'at the end of the day Shadwell called to one of the riders saying, "Put thickey hoss into a trot and see". In a few steps the outhurler overtook the rider and vaulted onto the horse behind the saddle and off they rode together to Brandis Corner where all sat down to a much needed supper at the Bickford Arms'.

A sport which is recorded is cricket. The Dickinson family at Dunsland were enthusiastic cricketers. Harvey Dickinson played for the county, and in the summer holidays after the

Above: Hounds meeting at Bovacott with F.M. Saunders and Phil Back (standing) and Thomas Kivell (mounted second from the right). October 1938.

Below: The Devon Ramblers Cricket team, 1938, with Harvey and Bickford Dickinson (top left and bottom right) Also in picture : Bob Kivell, the Rossiter twins from Hatherleigh, the Revd. R. Holmes from Monkokehampton, and W. Rowland.

First World War, when the three boys were either at school or university they organized a touring team (the Devon Ramblers) which played all over Devon. Between the wars there was regular village cricket. Every Saturday afternoon, unless harvesting made it impossible to raise a team, Bradford played cricket, at home or away, against a neighbouring village. The home pitch was at Newbridge Park, Dunsland. Only the 'square' was roped off - the rest of the field was grazed by cattle until the day of the match. After the Second World War cricket was resumed, playing on a field behind Glebelands, between the Rectory and the church. A village football team was also formed in these years, organised by Bill Isaac, senior, who franticly rushed about most Saturdays in season trying to find enough players. They played for many years in the field adjacent to Fore Street and occasionally on the field beside the school.

Between 1987 and 1999 Jane Francis and her sister, Sara Osborne, organised a number of Pony shows, either at Bason or Glebelands.

Meet of the South Tetcott hounds at the Bickford Arms circa 2005.

15

WARS

During the first world war thirty three men were recorded as having served with the armed forces; six in the Royal Navy and twenty seven in the Army. Five names are recorded on the 1914-18 War Memorial in the parish church. They are:

Walter Evelyn Martin, the youngest son of George and Elizabeth Martin of Kenneland. He was a corporal in the Devonshire Regiment and died in the Middle East on 8th March 1916 aged 32.

Samuel John Sanders, the eldest son of John and Alice Sanders of Henscott Cottage. He was a private in the Machine Gun Corps and died in France on 27th July 1917, aged 26.

Percy Isaac, son of Frederick and Mary Isaac of Hollacombe who was a private in the Devonshire Regiment. He died in France on 15th October 1917, aged 21 years.

William Thomas Short, son of William and Minnie Short of Bideford. He lived with his wife Eva at Highstead Cottage. He was a sapper in the Royal Engineers and died in France on 11th April 1918 aged 35 years.

Stanley Albert Alford, nephew of Caris Sanders the widow of Samuel the blacksmith at Brandis Corner. He was a private in the Gloucestershire Regiment, and died in France on 4th November 1918 aged 19.*

In the Second World War such records as there are concern the Home Guard. They met at the Rectory barn (the church

---

* The names of those men from Bradford and Cookbury who served in the 1914-18 war are listed in appendices 10 and 11.

101

hall) under the command of Capt. Norman Kellaway of Fernlea, assisted by Sergt. Horace Skinner. There were search-lights stationed at Brandis Corner and near New Inn in Shebbear. Later in the war the Americans had a camp at Dunsland Cross during the build-up for D Day.

In 1937 'Master' Bickford Dickinson was invited to brief the Parish Council on air-raid precautions (he was now 37 years old, but referred to as 'master' while his father still lived). In 1940 the Rural District Council supplied sand for fires caused by bombs. Supplies were sent to Brandis Corner, Hole Moor, Priestacott and Middlecott Cross and the air raid wardens were to ensure that each house had a bucketful. Also in June 1940 the Council arranged for the collection of waste paper, Mr. Codd providing a collecting point at his shop. In July arrangements were made for the collection of scrap iron to be deposited at Bramble Quarry or Brandis Corner. Mr English made arrangements for the mill-wheel from Bradford Mill to be sent for scrap at this time.

There is little surviving documentation of the numbers of evacuees at Bradford during the Second World War, but eighteen of the Fenwick family, comprising three generations, came in June 1940. At first they lived in the kitchen quarters of Dunsland. Nine cousins went to Brandis Corner, Quick Mill and Shorts Farm. Two brothers and their grandparent were at Priestacott where Miss Stephanie English bought the elder boy a bicycle so that he could ride to Holsworthy School. Margaret Fenwick and her mother lived with Mrs Candler at Church Cottage. Margaret Daniels (née Fenwick) wrote in 1990 that she 'never felt unwelcomed or unwanted', and remembered collecting milk from Sanders' farm, visiting Codd's shop, and watching the blacksmith who read the Bible in the Methodist Church (William Reed).

Mrs George Candler (right) at Church Cottage with her sister-in-law, 1942

16

THE CHURCH IN THE 20th CENTURY

In 1905 a new organ replaced the old harmonium, but after twenty five years it is said that the Rector, Claud Williams, dismantled the organ and could not put it together again! Mr Williams came to Bradford in 1915, and in 1925 he also had charge of Hollacombe. The two parishes remained united until 1947, when Hollacombe was moved to the care of the Rectors of Holsworthy.

In 1932, after Mr Hustwayte became Rector, it was decided to improve the old rectory barn which had for some years been used, but not very successfully, as a parish reading room. During this time it had continued to be used for parish functions and for playing skittles. Money was raised by dances, whist drives and other activities and the work was done: a new floor was laid, cloak rooms were provided, and a new billiard table top was purchased. The work was carried out by Messrs Wm. Hopper, carpenter, William Heard, mason, and Leslie Parsons at the cost of £85.11s. The new hall, to be known as the Bradford Church Institute, was opened on 8th November 1934. It still needed a ceiling for the main hall and a porch for the south entrance, and there was hope of laying a concrete skittles floor. Mrs Hustwayte got together a group of players who called themselves The Bradford Barnstormers. There is a record of them presenting four short plays on two nights in April 1936.

In that year the church roof began causing some anxiety as plaster kept falling from the ceiling, and it was decided to put asbestos sheets over the plaster to prevent further trouble. Mr Hopper was engaged to do this for £45. Mr. Hustwayte also removed the old organ which his predecessor, Claud Williams, had dismantled but had been unable to re-assemble.

In 1952 Bradford was held with the parish of Thornbury when Maurice Comeau was instituted Rector, although he moved into residence the year previously. His father, Percival Comeau was Rector of Black Torrington from 1949–59. On the day of the Queen's coronation in June 1953 a united service was held in Bradford School at 2 in the afternoon to celebrate the occasion, and Col. Micholls presented the church with the flag of St George. Later that year a gift of oil lamps for lighting the church was received from the church of St Andrew, Sutcombe. In 1955 the tower was re-pointed and new lead laid on the tower roof. Maurice Comeau left Bradford for Yealmpton in 1957.

The Revd. Fred Pennington was instituted as Rector in May 1958. In November the church was connected to the mains electricity and new lighting was installed. At the dedication service on 23rd November the address was given by the Rev. Bickford Dickinson, who had just been ordained by the Bishop of Exeter and was serving a curacy at Holsworthy

Rev. Fred Pennington and his wife Dorothy with their children: Janet, Bill and Pamela in 1964.

before being appointed Rector of Lew Trenchard in 1960: thus following in the footsteps of his grandfather, Sabine Baring-Gould. Bickford had been teaching at Shebbear College before he was ordained.

In 1961 Mr Pennington persuaded the Diocese to convey the Church Institute and the land around it to the Parochial Church Council to be used as a church hall, and in 1968 it was connected to mains water. By 1978 the Church Council found that the cost of maintaining the building was beyond their means and the Diocese sold it to trustees on behalf of the Parish Council to be a Village Hall.

The Revd. Ron Baker became Rector of Bradford and Thornbury in 1967. He was an enthusiastic bell-ringer and organised the restoration of the bells in 1974-75, at a cost of £600. The belfry floor was replaced in 1968 and the tower parapet had to be re-pointed in 1977, which, together with patching part of the tower roof, cost nearly £2,000. The service to commemorate the Queen's silver jubilee that year filled the church, with, seemingly, most of the parish attending. Mr. Baker was the last Rector to live in the Rectory. It was sold by the Diocese at auction in July 1975 and in September Ron Baker moved to the new Rectory at Black Torrington. A united benefice of Black Torrington, Bradford and Thornbury had been formed in 1973.

The Revd. Gerry Matthews was appointed priest-in-charge of the three parishes in 1978 and retired in 1990. In 1982 St John's Cookbury was detached from Holsworthy and became a daughter church of All Saints, Bradford. At the same time the parish of Highampton was added to the benefice. In 1986 James Paterson, of Bideford, was commissioned to design a stained glass window for the south aisle in memory of Mildred Trible of Henscot, who had been churchwarden for a number of years. This was installed by Robert Paterson shortly after his father's death.

From 1991, in aid of church funds, Jane Francis produced versions of Shakespeare's plays on the old Rectory lawn, by kind invitation of Mr and Mrs John Granger. They began with scenes from 'Midsummer Night's Dream' and ended with a shortened version of 'The Tempest' in 1999.

Above: 'As You Like It' dress rehearsal in the Rectory garden 1995. Kathy Pole (Rosalind), David Broan (Oliver), Mollie Moppett, Gerry Matthews (Jaques), Jane Francis (Le Beau), John Moppett and Freda Broan (Touchstone).

Below: Congregation at Bradford Church on Mothering Sunday 2009. Back row: David Arney, Tony Lobley, Mary Keen, John Smale, Maurice Keen. Centre: Liz Priest, Helen Heard with Sam, Bob Clark, Lorna Harris, Eileen Arney, Alice Durrant, Mr Durrant with Louis in arms, Emma Durrant, Stan Bird, Marjorie Smale, Gina Finch, Edith McLeod and Margaret Taylor. Front: George Heard, Hazel Durrant, Nick Finch, William and Laura Priest and Roman Durrant.

17

BRADFORD CHAPELS

Rehoboth Chapel at Holemoor was built for the Bible
Christians in 1839 on land owned by Arscott Venton,
who also at this time owned all of Bennetts Hole. The
Bible Christians were a group who separated from the
Wesleyan Church in 1815 and formed their first society in
Shebbear. In the beginning they were led by William O'Bryan.
In 1907 they united with other separated Methodist groups
and in 1932 reunited with the Wesleyan and Primitive
Methodists to form the Methodist Church that we know
today. Rehoboth Chapel had a small graveyard attached and
a Sunday-school room was added later. In the religious
census of 1851 the Bible Christian minister of Shebbear, Jacob
Prior, recorded Sunday afternoon and evening congregations
of over 100, with the Sunday School meeting in the morning.
In the second half of the 19th century most of the population
of Holemoor seem to have been chapel-goers. The chapel was
closed in 2007.

A Wesleyan chapel was built at Brandis Corner in 1854 but
it was closed in 1983. Another Bible Christian chapel, Zion
Hill, built at Cookbury in 1840, closed in the 1990s.

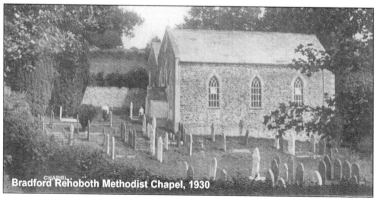

Bradford Rehoboth Methodist Chapel, 1930

Cookbury

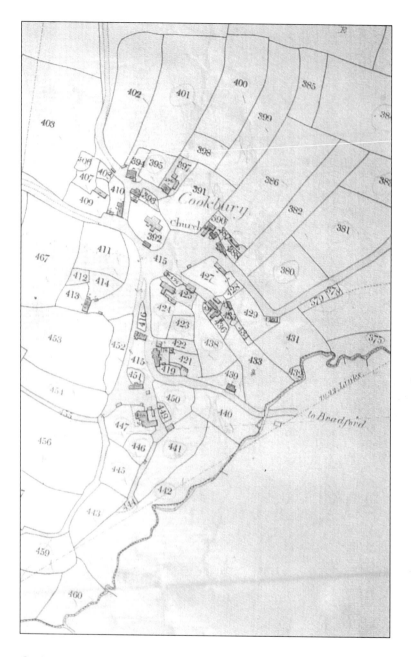

Cookbury Town from the Tithe Map of 1843

18

MANORS, FARMS & TRADES

The civil parish of Cookbury, now united with Bradford, takes its name from Cucca, a Saxon leader who made a settlement here. In the Domesday Book it is recorded as the Manor of Cookbury Wick (*Wicha*). It was held in the time of King Edward the Confessor by Wulfrun, a free woman, and granted by King William the Conqueror to Robert d'Aumale, a minor baron, who also held, among other places, Milton Damerel.

Stapledon Manor is first recorded in the Feet of fines for Devon in 1228. It lay somewhere between the present Stapledon farm and Upcott. The most famous member of the family was Walter de Stapledon born in 1261. He became professor of Canon Law at Oxford and chaplain to Pope Clement V. In 1307 he was made Bishop of Exeter. In 1315 he probably stayed at Stapledon with his brother Sir Richard when he came to rededicate the church. Sir Richard was a judge of the King's Bench, and member of Parliament for Devon in 1314 and 1319. Down the centuries the manor descended through the families of Hankford, St Leger, Speccott, Hele, Trelawney, May and Harvey. Mrs Henry Harvey was the last known holder of the lordship in 1926.

Wick Manor would appear to have become extinct several centuries ago. Richard Polwhele wrote that the buildings of Cookbury were mostly of mud and thatch. In 1797 he recorded that there were 12 dwellings in Church Town (around the church), 6 at Cookbury Week, 5 at Upcott and 3 each at Halsdon and Stapledon. The population of Cookbury in 1801 was 261. The two major estates in Cookbury are Halsdon and Upcott, both first mentioned in 1242. In 1850 most of Halsdon, 350 acres, was farmed by Richard Sanders. At the same time Upcott, 250 acres, was farmed by John Penhale whose grandson founded the veterinary firm of Penhale (now Penbode) in Holsworthy. William Ward farmed 200 acres at Stapleton, William Harris had 180 acres at Vaglefield farmed by David Hole, and Matthew Hole farmed 100 acres at Cookbury Week. By 1880 William Trible of Marhamchurch was farming Halsdon, having moved from Bagbeer in Thornbury with his wife Fanny and son Abraham, who, like his father, was a well known cattle breeder. He bought Henscott in Bradford in 1914, but he himself stayed at Halsdon. His son moved into Henscott in 1930, where the family stayed for over 70 years. Philip Venton was farming at Cookbury Wick in the 18th century. His son Philip married Grace Penwarden in 1822, and no doubt they could be linked to the Bradford Ventons.

There used to be an inn at Cookbury near the church. This was the New Inn, now called Oaklands Farm, where the Penwardens were landlords for two generations between 1840 and 1890. The last landlord was Samuel Jeffrey who held the licence in 1902. Robert Jeffery was granted a licence to sell beer and cider in Cookbury in 1731 but it is not known where the beer-house was. The Heysetts, who lived at Hollow Lakes in Cookbury Town, down 'Ramally Lane', were shoemakers for two generations in the 19th century; a son, Robert jnr., farmed at Wick into the 20th century. The Stidwells were carpenters (and masons) in Cookbury village for most of the 19th century; and the Gilberts, who were established in Cookbury in the 18th century, were blacksmiths and moved to Holemoor before the end of the 19th century. John Sanders who married Ann Gilbert in 1841 was a wheelwright and carpenter at Cookbury *Weeke* in 1850. 'Sanders' was a very common name in Cookbury and Bradford at this time. In the nineteenth century the population of Cookbury fell by 50%, from 300 in 1850 to 150 in 1900 and by 2000 it had fallen to 130.

Cookbury Church in 1992.

Matilda Ley ('Aunt Mill') of High Park Cottage, on her 100th birthday.
27th October 1985.

19

COOKBURY CHURCH

Although close to Bradford, Cookbury church was attached to Milton Damerel for many centuries until 1956 when it was united with Holsworthy. Much restoration work was carried out during the next three years to the roofs and guttering. In 1981 the church was declared redundant. However the parish was transferred to Bradford. It was reopened in 1987 as a chapel-of-ease to All Saints and more restoration work was done, particularly in re-slating the roof. It is basically a Norman church and much of the masonry in the nave and the chancel is Norman. The font has a square bowl with incised mouldings set on four colonnettes and is thought to be 13th century . The stonework of the east window is believed to be of a similar date.

The building was rebuilt, restored or enlarged early in the 14th century and was rededicated by Bishop Walter de Stapledon in August 1315.

The dedication to St John the Baptist and the Seven Maccabees is rare. There are a few churches dedicated to Old Testament saints but this dedication to the seven martyred brothers (2nd Book of Maccabbees, in the Apocrypha, Chapter 7) is unique in England.

The north aisle was probably added at the end of the 15th century and the arcade in the centre of the church is of this Perpendicular period. The pulpit is Jacobean and reputed to have come from a Launceston church (possibly St Thomas) which was being restored in the 19th century.

Richard Polwhele in 1797 wrote that the Bickford family of Dunsland had the right to seats in the south wing of the south aisle of the church. They were apparently given the use of two

Tenor bell in Cookbury church, 1668.

Above: Elizabethan Chalice and Paten made by Ions of Exeter 1577

Below: Drawings of 17th. century floor tiles, on the chancel floor, made from Fremington clay in Bideford or Barnstaple

pews in what is now known as the Dunsland aisle after the family gave the three acre Church Meadow to the church living. In 1638, and again in 1663, the Bickfords were granted a licence by the Bishop to attend Cookbury church rather than their parish church of Bradford. Polwhele noted that there was then a very small parsonage house by the churchyard. It provided a stable for the Rector of Milton Damerel when he rode over to take services. In the 20th century it became the church room. As well as being used for meetings, whist drives which were very popular were often held there. It was sold in 1981 and re-built as Glebe Cottage.

The church registers for baptism and burial are extant from 1746. There are a few marriage records from 1750; these are continuous from 1813. Walter Elford, Rector of Milton Damerel, signed the registers from 1752-1770. Walter Elford gave a 7 inch silver paten to the church in 1770, and in 1779 he bequeathed a 13 inch high domed silver tankard for the communion wine. By 1802 Thomas Clack was Rector, and he was followed in 1852 by William Anderson who remained at Milton until 1897. Robert Blight is recorded as Churchwarden for Cookbury in 1825, and John Sanders and Philip Venton in 1829.

The church was restored in about 1870 when the oak screen was erected and the eagle lectern was installed on an earlier base. The stained glass in the east window, and other windows, is by Beer of Exeter and was inserted about the same time. The treble bell, which is cracked and stands on the floor of the church, was cast in Exeter in 1570. The tenor bell alongside it was also cast in Exeter (by Pennington) and is dated 1668. The bell hanging in the tower is also 17th century. In the church there is a memorial to those of the parish who were killed in the First World War. These were:

Stanley Thomas Nicholls, the younger son of George Nicholls of Holemoor, was a private in the Devonshire Regiment and died in France on 6th September 1916, aged 24 years. (George Nicholls was a Bible Christian lay preacher and Sunday-school teacher. The congregation at Holemoor chapel gave Mr Nicholls a finely bound Bible for use in the pulpit in memory of his son Stanley).

Herbert John Brock, the son of John and Brida Brock of Shebbear, was also a private in the Devonshire Regiment who died in France on 23rd April 1917, aged 22 years.

Heber Percival Hayman, a private in the Gloucestershire Regiment, was the younger son of Lewis and Clara Hayman of Halsdon Cottage. He died in France on 31st May 1918, aged 21 years.

After Cookbury Church was transferred to the care of Bradford in 1987 efforts were made to do some repair and restoration, and to re-slate the entire roof. The cost was estimated at £40,000 and a grant was received from English

13th century font.

Heritage of £24,000. With other grants and fund-raising the work was completed and the church was rededicated by the Bishop of Plymouth on 21st June 1992.

On 15th December 2005 the Revd. Kathy Roberts was licensed as priest-in-charge of the United Benefice: the first woman priest to officiate in Bradford and Cookbury.

Cookbury flower festival, June 1988

Re-dedication of Cookbury Church after restoration June 1992.
John Granger, Gerry Matthews, Sarah Baker, Richard, Bishop of Plymouth, and John Smale.

20

ENVOI

Time passes: people come and they go: children are born, and either as children or adults they die: houses are built, some are enlarged, some decay: some of these events pass into history and some are forgotten, others become fable or legend or get mixed up with different events. I have tried to discover the history and to preserve known facts as much as possible. Sometimes records of past events are found after having been long hidden or relics are unearthed which shed new light on the past and our understanding of history may have to change. I have endeavoured to tell the past as accurately as I can. I present this history, not as infallible, but as near to the truth as I can make it with a belief that the past is important in understanding the present and hoping that we in our turn may lay good foundations for the future.

I conclude with a poem written by Bickford Dickinson, who for twenty five years lived at Dunsland. He was successively school master and parish priest. The poem was written on his retirement as Rector of Lew Trenchard in 1965.

The Three Loves

1918-38. I gave my youth to the home I love,
The old grey house that my fathers raised.
I squandered my strength in the years I strove
For the dear green fields where the cattle grazed.
THOUGH I LOST THE LOT OF THEM, WHY REPINE?
FOR DEEP IN MY HEART THEY ARE ALWAYS MINE.

1945-59. I gave my mind to the boys I know,
The loud-voiced lads with their lives ahead,
I saw them come and I watched them go
To fight life's battles when I am dead.
AND SOME WIN FORTUNE AND SOME WIN FAME
DID I HELP TO TEACH THEM TO PLAY THE GAME?

1959- To the Church of God I must give my heart,
But now there is little that's left in hand,
When youth and vigour and health depart;
Yet somehow I think He will understand
THREE THINGS WHICH FOR ME ARE OF UTMOST WORTH
THE CHURCH, GOD'S CHILDREN AND ENGLISH EARTH.

Appendices

APPENDICES

1. Rectors and Patrons of the Parish of Bradford.

Date of appointment	Rector	Reason for vacating the benefice	Patron
1309	William Mewy		
1321	William Basset (or Russel)		John Denys
1335	Hugo de Gretton		John Denys
1349	John Sampson	exchanged	John Denys
1354	John Knythe	resigned	John Denys
1357	William Portejoye	exchanged	John Denys
1363	Roger Langtre	died	John Denys
1412	John(or Richard) Penells, LL.D.	resigned	Isolda, widow of Walter de Denys
1416	John Wolston	resigned	Isolda Wybbury née Denys)
1418	James Carslegh, LL.B.	exchanged	Isolda Wybbury
1419	Geoffrey Veale	exchanged	Isolda Wybbury
1422	John Alnethcote	resigned 1432	Isolda Wybbury
1450	Hugo Froster, a monk	resigned	Gilbert Denys
1455	Thomas Burton	exchanged	Gilbert Denys
1459	Adam Rawe	exchanged	Gilbert Denys
1459	Josias(or William) Kene		Gilbert Denys
?	William Pyerce	died	
1528	Thomas Browne	resigned	William Gifford de Yeo

Year	Incumbent	Status	Patron
1552	John Arscott	died	John Arscott of Tetcott & Richard Cavell, by grant of John Gyfford
1557	Simon Atkyn, D.D., S.T.P	died	John & Wilmota Bury
1560	William Cavell, M.A.	died	John & Wilmota Bury
1591	George Close, M.A.	deprived	Sir George Cary
1615	Thomas Saltern, B.C.L.	died 1652	Sir George Cary
1657	John Tooker	died	Sir George Cary
1699	Josias Richards, M.A.	resigned	Edward Cary
1704	John Silke, B.A.	died	Richard Osborne
!719	Robert Brown	died	George Cary
1739	William Keate, jnr. B.A.	resigned	William Bampfield
1741	Gregory Tamlyn, B.A.	died	William Bampfield
1800	John Pearse Manley, D.C.L.	resigned	William Carslake
1803	John Bampfield, B.A.	died	William Carslake
1842	John Carslake Duncan Yule	died	Bampfield Trust
1885	Robert Lewis Bampfield, M.A.	died	Bampfield Trust
1888	John William Lewis Bampfield, M.A.	died	Bampfield Trust
1890	Francis Russell Rawes, M.A.	ceded	Bampfield Trust
1904	John McWilliams Bampfield, M.A.	ceded	Bampfield Trust
1911	John Henry Snow, M.A.	ceded	Bampfield Trust
1915	Claud Williams, M.A.	ceded	Bampfield Trust
1931	Herbert Leonard Hustwayte	ceded	Bampfield Trust
1937	Arthur Ernest Edwards, M.A.		Bampfield Trust
1946	Cyril Henry Donne, A.K.C.	resigned	Bampfield Trust
1949	George Lansdell Jarratt, M.A.		Priest-in-charge
1950	Edward Royle, M.A.		Priest-in-charge

1. Rectors and Patrons of the Parish of Bradford.

Date of appointment	Rector	Reason for vacating the benefice	Patron
1952	Maurice Aldham Paston Comeau, B.A.	ceded	Bampfield Trust
1958	Frederick William Pennington	ceded	Bampfield Trust
1967	Ronald Harry Baker	ceded	Bampfield Trust
1978	Gerald Lancelot Matthews	resigned	Priest-in-charge
1991	Howard John Mayell	ceded	Priest-in-charge
1997	David Michael Wood		Priest-in-charge
Rector from 2001		resigned	Diocesan Board of Patronage
2005	Kathleen Marie Roberts		Priest-in-charge

2. 1332 Lay Subsidy - Bradford List.
(Voted by Parliament for Edward III to fight the war in France)

Taxed @ 3/-	John Deneys John Cadie	Taxed @ 1/-	Richard De Heynstecote Thomas Fraunceys Robert Mareschal
Taxed @ 18d.	William de Ryghtodan Martin de Clauyle	Taxed @ 9d.	William Carpentar William Fullonere Reginald de Heynstecote John Hywyn
Taxed @ 15d.	John Floyer		

3. 1525 Devon Subsidy Roll.
(A tax to pay for wars in France and Scotland)

Land rates			
L 60	Humphry Batyn		
L 2	William Gerne		

Value of goods			
G 30	Richard Cavell	G 5	John Arscott
G 10	Thomas Scame	G 5	John Nucort
G 8	Stephen Colwyll	G 5	Walter Squier
G 7	John Persse	G 4	William Pyne
G 6²/₃	Joan Doun	G 4	John Donscombe
		G 4	Thomas Colwyll
		G 3	William Scame
		G 2	Baldwin Kyng

4. 1569 Devon Muster Roll.
(Preparation for defence against invasion)

Presenters for Bradford:	William Maynard	Stephen Roye.	
Assessed to provide arms on income from land of £20-40.	Elizabeth Fortescue (widow) John Henscott, (gent)		each to provide 1 corslet, 1 pike, 1 morion, 1 harquebus, 1 steel cap, 1 bow.
Assessed to provide arms on income from goods of £10-20.	Stephen Rowe, Robert Colwill Joan Colwill,widow, John Colwill		Each to provide 1 bow, 1, steel cap, 1 sheaf of arrows, 1 bill.

5. 1581 Devon Subsidy Roll.
(Tax to prepare for war with Spain)

Land Tax		Tax on goods	
L 10	John Arscott (armiger)	G 6	Thomas Northcott
L 8	Mrs Ellena Arscott, widow	G 4	Ema Whiet
L 5	Robert Cary, gent	G 3	Ralph Bond
L 5	Thomasina Maynard, widow	G 3	Richard Colwill
L 4	John Colwill	G 3	John Waie
L 3	Henry Huchines	G 3	John Hayne
L 2	Lewis Arscott	G 3	John Pruste
L 2	William Denynge		
L 1	William Robbine		

6. 1624 Devon Subsidy.
(Parliamentary Tax for James I war on Spain)

On land : Arthur Arscott, William Maynard, Christopher Maynard, Richard Gearne, John Anderton, John Hayne, Laurence Mudge.

On goods : Lewis Arscott, gent, Robert Colwill, Humfrey Waye, John Colwill, Richard Brawnde.

Cookbury –

On land : Richard Rolle, Humfrey Jeffery, Gideon Venton.

On goods Gregory Jeffery.

7.   1642   Tax Assessment.

Thomas Colwill	49/-	William Maynard	15/-
Thomas Salterne, clerk	46/8	George Risdon, gent	14/-
Sir Shilston Calmady	45/8	William Jeffery	12/8
Arthur Arscott Esq.	40/-	William Dennys	9/4
George Beare Esq.	22/4	Robert Cary, gent.	8/8
Richard Gearne	17/4	Sir Edward Cary, kt	8/8 *
John Colwill	17/4	Sir Nicholas Martin	5/4
Joan Parson	17/4		

*being a recusant convict & rated double

8.   1641.   Signatures to the Protestation.

Thomas Salterne,	Rector	Robert Jeffery,	Churchwarden
Richard Gearne,	Constable	Robert Jewell,	Overseer

Eelirzar Anderton	John Fynnamore	Robert Northcott
John Anderton	Jonas Fynnamore	Nicholas Peace
Robert Anderton	Bartholomew Gawmon	William Peatherick
John Arscott	Richard Gearne, snr	Robert Pengally

8.   1641.   Signatures to the Protestation (continued).

John Beabor
Diggory Bearman
William Bickford, gent
George Brodford
Robert Browne
George Bryant
John Bullin
John Colwill
Peathevick Colwill
Richard Colwill
Thomas Colwil
Thomas Cottle
John Dennys
Walter Drew
John Furber
Henry Fylbert

Richard Gearne, jnr
Robert Gearne
Roger Hayne
Charles Hockedie
Robert Jeffrey
Robert Jewell
Nathaniel Gilbert
William Kinsman
John Leach
John Lile
John Lucas
John Marchant
William Maynerd
Richard Meager
Robert Marley
Humphrey Northcott

Thomas Perkins
Thomas Pounsfond
John Robins
Richard Robins
William Robins
William Roche
Simon Seller
Jonathon Squeire
George Steevens
Edward Streat
Christopher Smale
Robert Thomas
William Troughton
Andrew Wallize
John Way
Alan Worth

Note: Christopher Colwill bedridden & incapable of protesting
William Paddon deaf and unable to hear the minister pray the protestation.

Cookbury – signed by:
Nicholas Upcott, curate   Humphrey Gloine, churchwarden   William Sincoke, constable

9. Churchwardens for the parish of Bradford in the 18th century.

1701	Stephen Jeffery	1730/1	John Heysett	1767	William Venton
1702	Elias Leach	1732-4	William Rigsby	1768	George Ward
1703	Simon Smale	1735/6	John Venton	1769	John Arscott
1704	John Browne	1737	Saml.Brown & Gideon Jewell	1770/1	John Norcott
1705	Ardilla Bray	1738	Humphrey Braund	1772	William Trick
1706	Elizabeth Arnold	1739/40	Joseph Jeffery	1773	Thomas Borrow
1707	Thomas Jeffery	1741	James Ley	1774	William Quance
1708	John Tricke	1742	John Trick	1775/6	Thomas Venton
1709	John Gilbert	1743/4	Francis Gloyne	1777/8	John Sluman
1710	Peter Gilbert	1745	Daniel Batten	1779	William Rigsby
1712/3	Robert Gearne	1746-9	Arscott Bickford	1780/1	Samuel Ley
1714	William Bickford Esq	1750-2	Lewis Heysett	1782-5	Thomas Mayne
1715	John Ward	1753/4	William Andrew	1786	John Daniel
1717	John Browne	1755/6	Stephen Coham	1788	John Arscott
1718/9	John Braund	1757	John Batten	1790	John Arscott
1720-2	Samuel Ley	1758/9	Richard Finemore	1791-4	William Mason
1723/4	John Ward	1760	William Burdon	1795	John Arscott & Wm. Mason
1725	Elnathan Petherick	1761/2	Lewis Heysett	1796-9	John Arscott
1726	Edmund Collecott	1763/4	Thomas Jeffery	1800	Stephen Venton & Wm. Mason
1728	Richard Mayne	1765	John Hockaday		
1729	William Jeffery	1766	James Ley		

10.   Men of Bradford who served in the armed forces in the 1914-18 war.

NAVY

Lieut. Stephen English	H.M.S. Illustrious
Chief Petty Officer TH Leach	H.M.S.Temerair
Petty Officer TD Davies	H.M.S. Essex
Petty Officer A. Heard	H.M.S. Devonshire
Stoker T. Jeffery	H.M.S. Isis
Seaman F. Jeffery	H.M.S. Quail

ARMY

Lieut. T. Ashton	Royal Engineers
Lieut. A.H.S. Dickinson	R.N.D. Hussars
Lance Corporal E. Martin	6th battn. Devons
Instructor William Braund	2nd Life Guards
Trooper W.H. Northcott	R.N.D. Hussars
Trooper Alwyn Sluggett	R.N.D. Hussars
Private William Bond	D.C.L. Infantry
Private R. Jeffery	1st battn. Devons
Private T. Gilbert	2nd battn. Devons
Chauffeur R.Chave Parsons	Motor Transport Corp

ARMY

Private T. Glover	6th battn. Devons
Private W. Balsdon	6th battn. Devons
Private W. Sanders	6th battn. Devons
Private T. Balsdon	6th battn. Devons
Private T. Stacey	8th Div. R.S.Artillery
Private S. Sanders	R.N.D. Hussars
Private W. Jeffery	Nat. Reserve
Private W. May	Army Service Corps
Bethuel Hutchings	Cape Mounted Rifles
William Osborne	1st Canadian Contingent
Samuel Osborne	2nd Canadian Contingent
F. Kellaway	D.C.L. Infantry
Edward Kellaway	6th battn. Devons
Archibald Kellaway	R.N.D. Hussars
John Taylor	Motor Dispatch Rider
Austin Taylor	Motor Dispatch Rider
William Daniel	R.E. Canadian Cont.

11. Men of Cookbury who served in the 1914-18 war.

NAVY	E. Bassett,	F. Ham,	Harold J. Merryman.
ARMY	W. Blight,	F. Bailey,	Arscott S.H. Dickinson,
	Edward Dickinson,	Samuel Gerry,	H.C.F. Harvey,
	W. Hayman,	H. Hayman,	A. Hawkins,
	A. Heddon,	W. Jeffery,	E. Ley,
	S. Osborne,	F. Sanders,	G. Sanders,
	C. Sanders,	S. Sanders.	

12. Coham-Dickinson Family Tree.

William Holland **Coham** married Mary Bickford in 1790.
(1763-1825)

William Bickford **Coham** married Augusta Mary Davie Bassett in 1827.
(1793-1843)

William Holland Bickford Mary Bassett Eleanor Augusta Christiana Davie Arscott Courtenay Bickford
(1828-1880)   (1829-1863)   (1830-1901)   (1832-1873)
married Dora Elizabeth Scott marrd. William Parr married Harvey George **Dickinson**

Arscott William Harvey
married Mary Baring-Gould in 1893

Eleanor Mary Bickford
married Blyth **Fleming** in 1881

Blyth Bickford **Coham-Fleming**
(1885-1929)

Arscott   Edward   Bickford
                             (1900-1975)

Edward Gaskell
publishers
DEVON

INDEX

INDEX

INDEX

INDEX

INDEX

Edward Gaskell
publishers
DEVON